Being Saved

Michelle Royers

Copyright © 2024 by MICHELLE ROYERS

All rights reserved.

No portion of this book may be reproduced in any form without written permission from the publisher or author, except as permitted by U.S. copyright law.

Contents

1. Chapter One — 1
2. Chapter Two — 6
3. Chapter Three — 11
4. Chapter Four — 17
5. Chapter Five — 21
6. Chapter Six — 33
7. Chapter Seven — 43
8. Chapter Eight — 49
9. Chapter Nine — 64
10. Chapter Ten — 78
11. Chapter Eleven — 89
12. Chapter Twelve — 98
13. Chapter Thirteen — 104
14. Chapter Fourteen — 116
15. Chapter Fifteen — 125

16. Chapter Sixteen   136
17. Chapter Seventeen   147
18. Chapter Eighteen   159
19. Chapter Nineteen   169
20. Chapter Twenty   178
21. Chapter Twenty-One   189
22. Chapter Twenty-Two   202
23. Chapter Twenty-Three   211
24. Chapter Twenty-Four   224
25. Chapter Twenty-Five   232
26. Epilogue   240

Chapter One

It's dark outside, night-time. It is a little bit cold too, since it's pretty late. I can barely see anything out here, like always. There are no people around this forest; I haven't seen people for ages.

Mummy and Daddy still haven't come to find me yet. They will, though. They promised. They told me to hide and to stay as quiet as possible. Mummy explained to me that we are playing the silence game, like we do in the car sometimes.

The silence game is where I have to be as quiet as possible for as long as I possibly can. So far I am doing really well! I haven't said a single word yet!

But, I admit, after a while I got bored of the silence game and hiding. There was nothing to do! I wanted to go home and play with my dolls and my teddies! I want them to have a tea party in my doll house that Mummy got for me. I have this one cuddly toy of a grey wolf that I named Miah. She has shiny blue eyes too!

She's my favourite toy out of all of them.

So after I got bored I left my hiding spot and went looking for Mummy and Daddy. But I got lost and now I don't know where I am. I also lost track of time, so I don't know how long I have waited out here for my parents. It can't have been too long... right?

My clothes got too small for me very quickly, as if I had a growth spurt, so now I am in my wolf form always.

I can't remember my first and last name or address anymore. I forgot them. I don't remember anything of what my house or family looked like, and I can't remember if I had any friends or not. I can't remember what anyone looked or sounded like, only what they smelled like. I can't remember my name either. Did I already say that?

I guess I have a bad memory, since I can't seem to remember much of my life!

I do remember my older big brother, Jackson, though. We just call him Jack as a shorter nickname thing. Saying Jackson is too much of a mouthful. He is four years older than me, I think. I don't really remember what he looks like or what his voice sounds like, but I do know that he was a person in my life, my older brother.

He likes to push me down the stairs for fun, which makes me cry my eyes out because it hurts me when I fall. Every time I go up the stairs, either to go to my pink bedroom, the bathroom or maybe the toy room, no matter where I am or what time of the day it is, he is always there to push me around. He says its fun, which I don't get. How could pushing your little sister down the stairs be fun? That's just naughty, and he always gets in trouble. He never learns, though, because he always does it. Every single time.

I don't like Jack very much; he's too mean to me.

I remember that the last time I saw my parents I was six years old. Which means I'm still six, right? That means I am a big girl now. Although Jack says I'm still a little baby because I still cry when I get hurt and I still sometimes have nightmares.

After Mummy and Daddy left me to hide, they left in werewolf form. I don't know where Jack is hiding, or even if he was playing our game with Mummy and Daddy.

But there were lots of loud bangs, so I stayed quiet like Mummy and Daddy told me to. I always do what Mummy and Daddy says, because if I don't that means I'm being naughty. I'm a good girl, I like to be praised. It makes me feel happy.

I remember that sometimes if I was a good girl, Mummy would play with my hair at night. She would braid it into an elaborate braid and because I had long hair that was a good thing. It was Mummy and me time. Just the two of us while Daddy and Jack did some boy stuff. I never really liked doing boy stuff, it's not girly enough.

But now I am lost.

I yawn, say excuse me in my head to be polite, and stretch like a cat I once saw prowling around our huge house. I stand up from my comfy spot under a tree and start towards where I know I can find something to eat.

Loping through the trees, I head towards a small clearing that has long tickly grass that always brushes against my legs. Clusters of clover are all through it which attracts wild... furry brown bunnies!

They are very cute, but I am hungry and they taste nice. Plus once when I was being nice to a bunny, it bit me very hard on the nose! Rabbits aren't nice. But they are nice tasting. And because I am so small a single rabbit, maybe two, is enough food to fill my stomach for a day or two. But it depends on how big the rabbit is, and how much fat the rabbit has on its body. Cause with all its yucky fur and cotton ball tail, there might not be enough food to fill my empty belly.

As I approach the clearing, loud voices crowd my ears. Barks and yips of joy, natural wolf sounds that sound good and happy.

Fear jumps at my heart. But then excitement. Mummy and Daddy! Even maybe Jack! They took me to the clearing once! That's how I know about it.

With a loud, excited bark I race for the clearing, smiling my cute smile.

But when I bound into the clearing, jumping over the long grass, fear returns.

I am face by four large wolves, two brown with various white markings, one red and one a grey colourd one. My parents weren't that colour. Neither was Jack.

The four wolves stand up, hunching to their full height. They tower over me, a little more than twice my size.

I whimper in fear, lowing to the ground in a submissive stance.

The leader of the small group of wolves, the grey one, growls at me angrily. He obviously does not like being seen by me. Maybe they are bad rogues. My Daddy told me about that rogues that terrorize packs for no reason at all.

Daddy doesn't like rogues, so I don't like rogues.

I stand up to them, growling, but I sound like a baby puppy.

They laugh at me.

I growl, snapping my jaws threateningly.

That annoys them.

The grey wolf jumps at me, grabbing onto my front leg and yanking it out from under me.

A howl of pain comes from me, ringing up above the trees and scaring birds away.

I wrench my leg away, just as the other three come barrelling towards me.

Fear strikes at my heart again as I spin on my heels and bolt away from them, my tiny size working to my advantage so I can slip under logs easier. I hear the four rouges hot on my heels, scaring me into action.

I howl in fright again, calling for my Mummy and my Daddy. They will come and help me, because I am their daughter.

The red wolf jumps at me when I reach another small clearing surrounded by trees, tackling me to the ground painfully. I howl in pain again as my back leg bends under my painfully. I whimper as I feel the wolf's hot breath on the top of my head.

I try wriggling out from under him, but he stays snarling on top of me.

The red furred wolf wraps his jaw around my throat and squeezes. It makes a wheezy, raspy breath get forced out of my lungs.

I wait for my death.

Mummy is not going to like this.

Chapter Two

(Ashton's POV)

I watch my pack around the weekly bonfire we have with blank eyes. When I see a bunch of bullies cornering a little nerdy kid, I narrow my eyes.

A loud snarl erupts from my chest. "What do you think you're doing?" I snarl, standing and drawing myself to my full height, which I have to admit is quite a lot.

The entire bonfire goes quiet. The only noise audible is the crackling of the fire and the slight rustling of the trees.

It's late at night, dark too.

The three bullies cower under my hateful glare.

"N-nothing, alpha." One stutters.

I growl. "No lying." My voice comes out angry as my eyes darken slightly. "Leave the kid alone unless you want to get bullied yourselves." I snarl.

"Yes sir." Another mumbles, before all three of them scurry off. The kid they were going to beat up moves off to his little friends while I lean up against a tree, watching again. The bonfire is held in a large clearing to accommodate my large pack.

I inherited my pack when my father was killed by those damn pesky rogues. I hate rogues, everyone does.

"Hey, Ash." One of the pack girls, Hannah, purrs, latching herself onto my arm. It is obvious she wants to be with the Alpha.

I shake her off violently with a growl. "Get off." I growl.

I'm not interested in girls, especially not from sluts and boyfriend stealers. I couldn't care less about not having a mate, and I don't really want one. They would just tie me down and give me a weakness. I honestly don't want a mate.

I would probably reject her anyway.

That is my opinion on mates.

But you never know, I might end up liking her.

A piercing howl breaks through the calm fun of the night. It makes something inside of me stir with worry and anger.

"Alpha?" My beta, Joshua, asks me, stepping forward.

"You and two fighters follow me. Now." I exaggerate, glaring at him to enforce my seriousness. "Everyone else back to the pack house." I growl louder.

As another pained howl strikes my eardrums, panic starts to bubble in my chest. Whoever it is that is getting attacked they must be in serious pain.

Running off into the forest, I strip out of my clothes and shift into my enormous black wolf. Since I have alpha blood in me, my wolf is a little bigger and stronger than others. I scoop my clothes up in my mouth, before taking off towards the sound of the howls.

I push my paws faster than ever before, streaking towards the howls of pain.

I reach a meadow with long grass and clovers, and instantly the smell of rogues hits me. It reeks like dirty fur and blood.

I growl viscously.

Joshua and two other fighters appear behind me, growling equally as viscously as I am. Together we move towards the growls and snarls.

Then another scent hits me.

A... softer one. A scent that makes my knees threaten to collapse out from under me. It smells like soft soap and jasmine. It smells divine.

'Mate...' My inner wolf whispers protectively, perking up excitedly.

What?!

An instinct to protect whoever it is that belongs to this scent swells over me, blocking out all other rational thoughts as my wolf fights for control of my body. He wants to see his mate, and he wants to see his mate now.

With an angry roar I rear forwards, charging through the forest, growling.

I burst into a clearing to see three wolves, one grey two brown, circling around a red wolf. Underneath the red one is a tiny, tiny light blonde wolf with a white tipped ear.

'Protect mate!' My wolf roars.

I howl in answer.

Leaping at the red wolf, I wrap my jaws around his throat and shake him off the tiny wolf. Who knew wolves got that small?

Clamping my teeth around the rogues neck, I growl and shake my head, rearing up to throw him into a tree. He yelps in pain, staggering to his feet again.

But before he can shake away his dizziness, I jump at him and tear his throat out without a second thought. My wolf is half in control of my body, instincts to take his mate somewhere safe and away from harm.

Joshua and the other two fighters fend off two of the remaining three werewolves. They are much stronger than I thought they were.

When I turn back around, I see the grey wolf trying to drag my mate away while she struggles in his jaws weakly. She yelps in pain as his teeth dig into her skin.

That makes me snap.

With a furious growl I jump at him, wrenching my mate back with my front paws. The grey wolf jumps at me while I jump at him. With a snarl I duck under him and jump at his stomach, tackling him to the floor. I don't hesitate to rip his throat out, careful not to swallow any of his rancid blood.

I jump back away from his now limp body, breathing heavily.

I watch Joshua and the other fighters taking down the other two rogues, debating whether or not to help them speed up the process.

When I hear a tiny, tiny whimper and feel something small and soft crawl under my body quite easily, cowering between my front legs, my decision is made.

I crouch closer to the ground, forming a protective barrier over my small mate. Why is she so small? She seems smaller than a normal wolf, let alone a werewolf.

When Joshua and the two fighters finish off the two remaining rogues, I start to relax.

But it is short lived. What were rogues doing on my land? I haven't been bothered by rogues since my father and oldest sister were killed. So what are they doing back? And what is my tiny mate doing out in the forest alone? Is she a rogue werewolf? I casually sniff the fur on top of her head without her noticing. She doesn't smell like a rogue. But then why is she being attacked by rogues?

Joshua and the two fighters cautiously step closer. I see they have no wounds.

When Joshua comes closer again, my mate whimpers frightfully and wiggles out from under me. Quicker than I thought she could move, she bolts away from us.

A tiny whimper of dislike comes from me, followed by a protective growl to guard my mate.

I get up and run after her, determined not to let her get away.

I am so not giving my mate up that easily.

Chapter Three

(Normal POV)

I watched in fear as the four new wolves tore apart the rogues that were going to kill me. The biggest one, way more than twice my size, with the shiny black fur and alluring brown eyes that sparkled, was the one that saved me personally.

He killed the red wolf who was choking me, then killed the grey wolf who was the leader that was trying to drag me off. Kidnap me. Well, wolf-nap me.

I whimper as I watch the other two wolves fight some of the good wolves. My eyes flick towards the black wolf. He looks strong and brave, like my Daddy was when it came to me, my brother Jack and my Mummy.

The black wolf looks ready to spring back into action, but I want to run and hide. So I crawl across the ground and under him, cowering between his front legs with a frightened whimper. What if the two rogues are bad and strong and get past all the wolves, even the black one?

The black wolf growls protectively, crouching down above me so that he forms a barrier around my body. No part of my small frame can be seen through him, just my head pops out below his.

With wide eyes I watch the three good wolves fight the two remaining rogues.

When they kill him, I relax a little. They can't hurt me if they aren't breathing.

As one of the good wolves with dark brown fur steps forwards towards me, I whimper in fear. His gaze sweeps down towards my head, his eyes filled with a strange emotion.

I watch as he takes another step towards me, starting to feel threatened. I wiggle out from under the black wolf, surprising him.

Spinning on my heels, I turn away from the wolves and sprint away, whining in fear all over again. Are these new wolves going to eat me or kill me like the other ones were? Did they just save me so they could finish the job?

I hear paws racing after me, and instantly get a shot of energy. I race forwards, my only thoughts about getting away from the black wolf following me, until...

I smell a bunny!

Skidding to a full stop, I trod quietly up to a bush. Sticking my head through it, I take in a deep breath. I smell the very distinctive scent of a rabbit.

Pulling my head out of the bush, I creep around the side of the bush ninja style, like Jack once taught me to. I think he does it better than I do, though I'd never tell him that.

I am aware of someone watching me, the black wolf, but I ignore it. I go into hunting mode. I never did get to eat anything before I ran into the rogues path.

My eyes narrow in on the furry ball of fluff. Even though it is still night time, I can see perfectly fine. I sniff the air again, pin pointing the rabbit's position.

I crouch down, my butt higher in the air than my head. My back end wiggles with my tail down, like a cat would before pouncing.

I hear the black wolf chuckle behind me.

The noise he make's startles the rabbit. It bolts off into the undergrowth.

I spring into action. Jumping over the bush I was hiding behind with an excited yip, I streak after it. My small size helps me to slip under the smaller plants that I would have to jump over if I was bigger. I follow its scent right on the dot, picking up speed.

It makes sharp turns, but I pounce on it, slapping my two front paws over it to pin it to the floor in another small clearing with trees surrounding me. My butt sticks in the air as I pin the rabbit down with both my front paws, my tail wagging furiously.

I bark at the bunny. It struggles under my paws, scratching at me. I push down on its neck, snapping it in one fluid motion to make the rabbit feel as little pain as possible.

Scooping the rabbit up in my jaws, the sound of someone following me has me on alert again. Daddy always taught me to be careful of my surroundings.

I stand up straight, ears perked high, eyes wide and rabbit dangling from my mouth.

The black wolf steps out from the shadows, the moon reflecting off his shiny black fur. He watches me with his chocolate brown eyes.

Slowly, I blink once, waiting for his reaction. When he doesn't do anything, I chew down on the rabbit once, again waiting to see his reaction.

When he just watches me wild mild fascination, I grin to myself in my head. Maybe he's not going to eat me!

I snarl at my dead prey, jumping while twisting my body around and bucking out my feet. I flop onto the ground, chewing the rabbit without actually eating it just yet.

The black wolf bursts out laughing at my strange movements, a low coughing sound.

I start eating the fat rabbit, trying not to swallow any of its coarse fur. I learnt that the fur of a bunny doesn't taste very nice and is hard to swallow. I learnt that the hard way. Never again am I ever going to eat a rabbit with its fur still there. Yucky.

The black wolf steps closer, sitting two metres away from me.

I growl my little puppy growl, wanting to keep my food to myself. I killed the rabbit, so I get to eat the rabbit. That's what Mummy and Daddy always said. If you can kill it by yourself, you can eat it by yourself. Then it's fair.

The black wolf comes closer again, completely ignoring my warning growls like Jack always did.

I narrow my eyes at him, frowning. Why is he ignoring me? He is so big that my rabbit probably wouldn't even make a morning snack for him. Barely even a bite. But for me it makes half a proper meal because I am so small.

The big black wolf sits next to me on his haunches, towering over me. He watches me with his warm brown eyes, luring me into their deep depths...

With a shake of my head and a thump of my tail against the ground, I continue eating my rabbit. It tastes nice, plump and juicy.

When I finally finish my meal, my stomach feeling a little bit fuller than before, I stand up and stretch with a big yawn. Eating always makes me sleepy.

I start to head off towards my favourite sleeping spot, but the black wolf stops me. He steps in front of my path, his big body blocking my tiny one. I give him a look of complete confusion and slight annoyance. Why can't I go to my sleeping spot? I'm tired!

The wolf whines quietly, dipping his head to nudge me in the direction of the way he came from. I frown in confusion again. What does he want? The black wolf nudges me forward again, almost making me trip over with his strength. I step in the direction he tells me to go, wondering if that is what he wants.

The wolf follows me, nudging me again.

He wants me to go with him? Should I? Mummy and Daddy always say to not trust strangers. But this stranger did save my life... and what if more rogues come back? Then I would surely be killed. So if I do go with the black wolf, he can keep me safe for Mummy and Daddy when they come to find me.

I step towards the direction the wolf was nudging me on my own, wondering if I am going in the right direction. When the wolf grins a wolf grin at me, I feel a sense of pride. The wolf follows me, starting to lead the way.

His big, warm body presses up against mine, making me feel safer than before. He leads the way like he owns this forest, like he knows the way. He might know it. My Mummy and Daddy knew the way around it.

I follow the black wolf cautiously. I don't really know what's going to happen. I am nervous. My ears flick back and forth and my eyes dart around wildly. I don't want to meet any more rogue werewolves, they scare me a lot.

After half an hour, we are still walking. It is very dark out now, darker than it was before. I am guessing it is maybe around midnight, way past my normal bed time.

When the black wolf beside me gets all tensed us and starts growling, my attention peeks and I look at him warily. Did I do something wrong?

The black wolf moves his legs over my body easily, standing over me protectively, looking into the dark shadows. I see four dark blurs step out from the shadows, growling and snarling at my black wolf.

Two have grey fur, two have brown fur. They all are bigger than me, but not as big as the black wolf. I take a curious sniff of the air, and recoil when the yucky smell of rogues fills my nose. To me they smell like rubbish and Jack's dirty socks. Stinky.

The black wolf with me snarls warningly at them, telling them to back off. One of the brown ones snarls right back. He is obviously the leader of the small group. Why are there so many groups of rogues around here now? And why do they always seem to find me?

The black wolf growls as the brown, leading wolf lunges.

Chapter Four

I whimper as the black wolf hovering over me jumps to my protection. He lunges at the brown wolf, the two colliding in mid air with a big thunk. With snarls and growls, the two tumble around on the ground, snapping at each other's faces and throats.

I close my eyes with fear, cowering towards the ground and wishing for my Daddy... and the black wolf.

When something grabs me roughly by the scruff of my neck, I let out a long yelp of hurt. One of the grey wolves yanks me up from my safe spot on the ground, biting into me a little too hard, hard enough that he draws blood.

I hear a snap, and see the leader of this small band of rogues dead in the jaws of my black wolf. His gaze swings towards me, and his warm chocolate brown eyes turn bright molten yellow with rage. I whimper desperately at him, struggling in the jaws of the grey wolf, wanting the comfort the black wolf seems to give me.

My black wolf lunges at the grey wolf holding me up, shoving him off me violently. I drop to the ground and hear a faint snap come from my front paw. I howl in pain, realising that my paw is now broken.

Out of nowhere, four new wolves race into the clearing. They smell slightly the same, meaning they are from a pack. They smell kind of like the black wolf, so I know they are good wolves and not bad wolves.

As the good wolves take on the rogues, the black wolf rushes to my side.

He whimpers quietly, his eyes still bright yellow. My breathing starts to quicken as shock finally sets in. I want Mummy and Daddy!

The black wolf starts to lick the wound on my neck, but it only makes me whine in pain. It hurts! The black wolf nudges me and whines at me quietly, apologizing. It isn't his fault though, so he won't be in trouble.

The black wolf's head swivels towards the other wolves that are helping him fight off the rogues. A little conversation goes on with them, probably through mind-link. Daddy told me that mind-link is shared between a pack and their alpha, so they can communicate in wolf form. Then there is the private mind-link that mates share. Mummy explained everything about mates to me. I can't wait to meet my mate! But I think I am only six so I'm probably not going to meet him until later in my life, after Mummy and Daddy have come to get me from this forest.

The black wolf eventually nods. He reaches down to my tiny body and gently holds me up off the ground by the scruff of my neck. This time it doesn't hurt. He is very gently, unlike the grey wolf that injured me. He whines quietly, holding me up easily off the ground. I curl up in on myself like a puppy would do when their mother picks them up to carry them.

In one fluid motion, my black wolf bounds off into the forest with an eager desire to get away from the fight. I whimper a little. He easily carries me through the forest, running much faster than I ever could even with me in his jaws.

Around a minute later, he slows down. Bursting through a line of trees, I am faced with a huge house, much bigger than my old house. It is a two story house, meaning it has stairs. Jack is going to push me down the stairs again! I think tiredly. I hate being pushed down the stairs, it hurts.

The black wolf trots straight for the house, nudging the door open and taking me inside.

My body trembles as he carries me up the stairs swiftly, expecting a push or shove from Jack. But then I realised that Jack doesn't live here, so I relax a little bit. The black wolf turns down one of the many corridors, heading for one of the many rooms at his house.

When he reaches the room he was carrying me to, I notice the door is slightly open, probably so he can get in and out in wolf form. Speaking of which, he nudges the door open with one of his front paws and lopes in.

I whimper when my broken leg gives off a wave of pain. I know it needs to be set straight so it heals properly.

The black wolf enters the room further.

I swear my jaw drops to the floor. The room is really big! It has a huge, King sized bed right in the middle under a wide window. To the left is probably a bathroom. Mummy and Daddy had a spare bathroom in their bedroom. There is also a flat screen T.V and a chest of draws. There is a bookshelf in this huge room. On either side of the bed are two beside tables, one on each side. There are little lamps on them, too.

The black wolf rears up a little and places me on the bed, nudging my backside up. He sniffs my face, pressing his cold nose to my forehead. I stretch my broken leg out in front of me, whining in pain and squeezing my eyes shut a few times.

The black wolf nuzzles my face once with his one, and I do the same, before he darts out of the room.

A sudden feeling of loneliness washes over me without the black wolf in the room. I shuffle backwards until my back hits the headboard. I curl up in on myself, whimpering quietly. My leg hurts, more than the time that Jack pushed me down the stairs a little bit too hard.

I know it is broken, because once when I was four I broke my arm when I fell off the monkey bars at the park. It was the same kind of pain as now.

When a familiar scent washes up my nose, my ears perk up. My whimpering in pain doesn't stop; it's a natural instinct when I am hurting.

I know that scent!

When the bedroom door is opened and two males walk in, my eyes lock onto the one in the white doctor's coat.

My tail starts to wag as I stare at him. He looks a little different now, but I would know that scent anywhere!

Jack!

Chapter Five

Ok, I am so sorry about the long wait! I had a massive fight with my b*itch of a 'mother' and she kicked me out of her house so I live with my Dad know. She practically kidnapped my poor USB and held it hostage until my Dad went and got it, as well as my phone :(She still has the laptop, but I put a password on it so she can't get to it. Eh, who cares anyway?

The chapters are now TWICE as long as the ones before before, so I hope you readers appreciate that

Anyways...

Enjoy! xox

*

I start barking frantically, trying to stand but failing miserably. The male who I haven't even looked at yet comes closer, putting a hand on my back to keep me pinned down to the bed.

I let out a barking howl at Jack, excited.

"Rosy?" His jaw drops.

I howl again. Rosy is my name! My nickname! I only ever let my brother Jack call me Rosy! I remember now!

Rushing forwards, Jack wraps his arms around my neck and squeezes the air out of my lings, tears appearing in his eyes.

Wait. Tears? Did I do something wrong?

"I thought you died Rosy! I thought I was alone!" He cries into my fur.

But what about Mummy and Daddy? I want to ask him.

"You know her?" The second male asks defensively.

My gaze swings to him. He's tall and muscled, very tall and very muscled in fact. He has the same soft chocolate brown eyes as the black wolf does. He has tousled black hair that sticks up in every different direction and strong cheekbones that highlight his bright eyes.

He looks drop dead gorgeous, if you ask me.

"Of course I know her!" Jack snaps. "She's my baby sister!"

I bark at him angrily. I'm not a baby anymore! I'm a big girl now!

Jack gives me a weird look. "Where have you been?"

"You know she can't answer you. She's in wolf form." The second boy points out.

I nod my head in agreement, happy that Jack is being silly and I'm not. Of course I can't speak to him in wolf form, silly boy!

Jack glares at the handsome boy, tugging me away from him. I yelp when my leg creaks in pain. Jack stretches it back out gently. "Go and get her some clothes, Ashton. I'm going to splinter her leg." Jack says firmly.

Ashton narrows his eyes at Jack, growling threateningly. "Don't order me around, Jack." He growls.

I sense a fight coming on, and I don't like fight. As easily as I can I twist my shoulder around and put my head in Ashton's lap, without hurting my broken leg. I look up at him with pleading eyes. I need some clothes so I am not naked in front of boys. That would be so embarrassing.

Ashton looks at me with his weary brown eyes, seeming to have a little debate in his head. He sighs once, looking away. "Fine." He grumbles under his breath, standing up and exiting the room quickly without looking back.

Jack splinters my leg, getting his equipment out of a first aid kit he brought in.

"You will heal faster in wolf form, so try not to move around too much and be careful shifting back and forth. You're leg has a clean break with no splinters, so it should almost be completely healed." Jack says, nodding in satisfaction.

When did my silly brother get to be so smart?

I blink at him, not really understanding much of his smart person's talk.

Ashton comes back in with a small pile of clothes in his hands. "I don't know her exact size so I guessed." He says, his voice quiet but firm, leaving no room for arguments or comments.

Jack nods, and then pats my head a little. "Do you know how to shift back?" he asks, an easy yes or no question.

I shake my head. I haven't even ever tried to shift back into my human form because my clothes got too small and too dirty. Mummy won't be very happy when I tell her I lost my clothes. But I can't lie to Mummy.

That's a bad thing to do and I don't want to get into trouble. Getting into trouble is a bad thing. But it's funny when Jack gets into trouble.

Jack sighs at me.

Ashton sits by me on the bed, absentmindedly patting the fur on top of my head. A small purring noise comes from me as I lean my head into his palm, which seems to please him and makes him smile to himself.

"All you need to do is focus on walking on two legs. Remember what it is like to be human. Just block everything out and focus on human aspects." Jack says.

I nod hesitantly, though I don't really understand what he is talking about. I can't remember what it is like to be human. I forgot.

Jack stands and leaves the room, followed by Ashton who takes a little longer to leave than Jack, this time looking back at me once.

I shift onto the bed into a more comfortable position. My leg isn't hurting as much now, I can feel it healing.

Closing my eyes, I think about what Jack says.

I think about walking on two legs instead of four. It's hard, since I have been in wolf form for a while. I don't know how long, just a while.

Then I think of human traits. Two eyes. Two ears on the side of your head. A mouth and nose in front of your eyes. Two arms. Two hands. Two thumbs. Two feet. Two legs. No tail. No claws. Normal teeth. Lowered senses.

After a moment of thinking about humans, I hear a few cracks. I cry out in pain as my body changes back into my human form. My bones all crack as my fur and claws retract. My pink skin replaces my fur. It's strange to look at, and I don't like it.

As quickly as I can I pull on the clothes at the end of the bed. Underwear that are white and fit alright. A pair of loose fitting pyjama pants that don't fit at all; they are too big. Then a white singlet that fits, but is a bit tight.

I crawl up to the headboard, bringing my knees up to my chest at the corner of the bed. I rest my chin on my knees, trying not to cry. Crying is bad. It makes my eyes all red and puffy.

I hold my broken arm in front of my chest, keeping it straight.

Jack and Ashton come back into the room.

Both stop to stare at me with wide eyes and dropped jaws.

I shrink away from their stares, feeling self conscious. These clothes don't fit me properly, and I haven't brushed my hair. It's all frizzy and wild. Plus I bet I'm covered in dirt and I smell.

That just makes me want to cry ever more.

"Rosy?" Jack whispers quietly, looking me over. He comes to the side of the bed and hugs me. I shrink into his chest, seeking comfort. His familiar scent clouds my senses for a brief moment.

Ashton climbs onto the bed on my other side, putting his hand on my back gently.

"Ok, Rosy. I'm going to ask you a few easy questions, ok?" Jack asks.

I nod, leaning back from him.

Jack sits in front of me. "Do you know what day it is?" he asks me.

I attempt to speak, but end up coughing. Ashton pats my back gently.

I try speaking again. "I don't know." I croak out, my first words for a while. I frown a little. They don't sound right. They sound older than I actually am.

"Do you know what year it is?" Jack asks me next.

I shake my head. "No."

"Do you know when your birthday is?"

"I can't remember." I admit.

"Do you know your name?" he asks.

"Rosy." I say.

"Your full name." Jack clarifies.

"I don't remember." I shake my head, a sinking feeling in my chest.

Jack's eyes widen. "Ok then. Do you remember your favourite colour?"

I shake my head.

"Your favourite toy?"

"Oh, that one is easy." I brighten up. "Miah is my favourite toy. My wolf with the crystal blue eyes." I grin happily; glad to answer at least one question.

Jack nods, a look of relief coming over his face.

"Do you remember how old you are?" He ask me.

I nod. "I'm six." I say.

Jack's face falls. "No, you're not six anymore Rosy." He says.

I frown in confusion. "No, I am six. I was six when Mummy and Daddy left me in the forest. We were playing the silence game, and I was winning." I grin happily again.

Jack shakes his head, tears filling his eyes. "You're not six, and I'm not ten anymore Rosy." He says quietly.

"I am six." I say forcefully, glowering at him.

"Rosy, you're not six. You're sixteen. You were out in that forest for ten years."

I faint.

"Rosy, wake up." A soft but firm voice whispers near my ear.

I startle awake, a frightened yelp coming from me. Where am I? Where is Mummy and Daddy? Why am I in human form?

I am greeted by two beautiful chocolate brown eyes that are twinkling like shining stars. They are familiar, I remember them. They belong to the handsome boy. I think his name was Ashton. That is a nice name, I think, I quite like it. A lot, in fact.

"Ashton?" I mumble weakly, struggling to sit up with a slight frown on my face. That is his name, right? Did I remember correctly?

A completely adorable grin spreads across his face, making his eyes shine even more. For some reason it makes my heart flutter.

"You remembered." He smiles at me, looping his arm under my back to help me sit up.

"Mmm..." I groan, my head pounding. Thoughts all crowd my mind.

My gaze swings to Jack, my brother.

"Ten years?" My voice comes out as a hoarse whisper.

Jack nods solemnly, reaching forwards the hold my tiny hands in his big ones. "You're not six anymore, Rosy, You're sixteen." He whispers.

I whimper. "Sixteen?" How can I be sixteen? "Why did Mummy and Daddy not come to find me?" I cry, tears clouding my eyes.

Jack stiffens.

I continue babbling on. "They promised they would come back! They promised!"

Jack gives me a look filled with sorrow. "Rosy, Mummy and Daddy aren't coming back. They passed away." He whispers.

My heart stops. Mummy and Daddy aren't coming back to get me? "Huh?" My bottom lip trembles as tears threaten to over flow from my eyes.

"Our parents passed away, Rosy. They died." Jack whispers.

My lip trembles again as ripping feeling tears through the centre of my chest, suffocating me under a sudden feeling of grief and sorrow. Mummy and Daddy can't have died! They promised to come and get me! They promised to find me!

"No!" I screech, throwing his hands away from mine and pushing myself backwards. "They're not dead! They can't be!" I start crying really hard, tears falling freely down my face. They sting a little.

Ashton growls at Jack threateningly, lowly, and I wonder why. Jack looks sad, guilty even.

"T-they can't be d-dead! No, no, no!" I scream at him hysterically, stuttering.

My body starts to shake as my wolf threatens to push out of my body and take control. She feels lonely, and doesn't like me being on two legs. It's too awkward and uncomfortable. Different from being on four legs.

"I think you should leave." Ashton growls forcefully at Jack, his voice full of authority. Is he an alpha like my Daddy was?

Jack narrows his eyes at Ashton and opens his mouth to say something, but a heartbroken sob comes from me, stopping him in his tracks. His eyes soften as they land on me, and he sets his lips in a thin line. "I'm sorry, Rosy." He whispers to me, before standing and exiting the room.

I burst into tears all over again. Now I've mad Jack sad! Is he angry at me? Why do I always do the wrong thing?

As a fresh flow of tears flood down my cheeks, and I feel like giving up. Mummy and Daddy aren't ever going to come and find me. I was out in the forest, lost, for ten years. I'm not six. I'm sixteen.

With my thoughts stuck on the devastation that has become my life, I completely forgot about Ashton still being in the room.

When I feel his big, soft hand touch my shoulder, as light as a feather, I jump a little. His strong arms snake around my skinny waist and easily lift me up as if I were lighter than air. His legs are crossed on his bed, his arms around me now. He holds me in his lap, my side against his warm chest. My head ends up in the crook of his neck.

(Ashton's POV)

I snake my arms around her slim waist, feeling overly protective of her. My wolf absolutely hates seeing her cry. He wants her to be happy, not upset.

Rosy. What a perfect name for her.

After she has managed to shift back and Jack and I had walked back into the room, I can't believe what I saw curled up on my large bed.

She's a small girl, shorter than average height. Tiny compared to me. Very skinny, underfed. She needs to gain a bit of weight. Being out in the forest hasn't been good to her human form. She has long, very, very long, light blonde hair that is tangled and wild since she hasn't been I human form in ten years. She has a small, heart shaped face that suits her perfectly. Big, wide baby blue eyes that are lighter than the sky and stand out against her pale white skin stared back at me. Her cheeks are coloured a light rosy pink colour that make her name suit her even more. I wonder to myself what her full name might be.

I will have to ask Jack about that.

Another sob rips through my angel's chest, her body shaking and quivering.

I hold her closer, hoping my presence will calm her down.

She just found out she was ten years older than she thought she was, and that her parents died before she could say goodbye. That is something her young mind shouldn't be able to process easily. I most likely wouldn't have reacted well if I were in her situation, no one would.

I whisper quiet words in her ear in a soothing voice. As gently as I can I run the back of my hand down her cheek, afraid that if I touch her too roughly she will break. She seems so fragile, so small against my much larger frame.

Rosy cries and cries, letting out all her sorrow from losing her family and having her entire world flipped upside down. I feel her tears fall onto my shoulder as she cries.

Standing up, I keep a strong hold of Rosy. Quietly, I walk towards my separate bathroom. The door is slightly ajar, so I can easily get in even with me carrying my tiny mate. I flip the light switch on with my elbow.

Rosy looks around quickly, taking in her new surroundings with watery eyes that are still spilling torrents of tears.

Lightly, I sit her on the sink's edge comfortably. Grabbing a face washer, I run it under warm water for a moment. Then, as gently as I can, I wash her face, getting all the tears off.

She closes her eyes as the warm material slides over her soft skin. I take this time to admire her beautiful face. Long black eyelashes that frame her startling blue eyes. Her strong cheekbones that always have splashes of colour in them. Her perfect pink lips that look completely kissable.

Everything about her is gorgeous. Breathtaking.

I re-wash the flannel, warming it with warm water again. I clean her arms free of dirt next, making sure she feels as comfortable as she can in human form.

I throw the now dirty flannel into the dirty washing hamper, and grab a hairbrush out of the sink drawer. The hairbrush was my sister's. She died when my father died, when we were attacked by rogues. Diana was always brushing her hair, she said it was relaxing and calming to do in the quiet. I kept her brush because it meant so much to her, and I feel like that if I have it I still have a physical connection to her. Not just memories of her.

Picking Rosy up again, her legs by my side and my arms under her thighs, I carry her back into my bedroom, hairbrush in hand.

I sit her on the edge of my bed lightly, and notice her eyes are still closed in grief and great sorrow. I frown at her sadness. Without a word I move to sit behind her, letting my longer legs dangle off the bed on either side of her.

Gently, I start pulling out the knots in her hair with my hands, leaving the brush sitting beside me on the bed. I work the knots with my fingers, teasing them apart gently. After around twenty minutes, when it is smoother, I finally pick up the brush.

Gently I brush her hair, making it nice and straight and smooth. It seems a lighter honey blonde colour now, and is much longer too. It goes all the way down past her waist in soft ringlets. I've never seen blonde hair quite this shade; it would be absolutely impossible to replicate. It's too... amazing to look good on anyone but my Rosy.

After a long while, I set Diana's brush down on one of my two bedside tables quietly. I lean forwards a little to have a look at Rosy's expression. I can't help but smile to myself when I see it.

An utterly calm expression is smoothed over her beautiful face. There are no lines of worry or grief on her forehead, and her eyes are now closed peacefully with no tears flowing from them anymore. Her soft pink lips look even softer the usual. She looks completely at ease.

Thanks Diana.

With a quiet, adorable little mumble of strange words, Rosy leans back and nestles into my chest comfortably. She tips her head back onto my shoulder lightly, turning her face into the crook of my neck.

Within a matter of mere seconds my Rosy is fast asleep, her mouth partly opened as soft noises come from her.

How adorable is she?

Chapter Six

Yay, early upload! I was kinda bored so i decided to write this, and this is where it ended up! Comment and Vote!!

And since I don't have much to say....

Enjoy! xox

*

(Rosy's POV)

"Mummy used to do that, you know." I yawn after waking up still cuddled next to Ashton. He is very warm, very nice to sleep on. Better than the ground, I decide.

"Do what?" He asks me, his arms around my waist and his head resting on my shoulder lightly, his legs on either side of me still.

"Brush my hair." I answer with a smile aimed at the wall in front of me.

"Oh, really?" He asks, genuinely curious, which makes me feel happier.

I nod eagerly. "Every Tuesday night. Sometimes when I was good she would at night, too." I explain matter-of-factly, nodding again.

Ashton smiles a little to himself, resting his chin on my shoulder again. "Maybe I could do that now?" He suggests hopefully.

I nod. "Yeah."

He smile widens. "Great."

I lean back against him, happy for the warmth he gives me. I am very small compared to him. Very small. He is very tall and looks very strong.

I try to keep my mind of my parents, but it is hard when everything reminds me of them. "Are my parents really gone?" I ask in a quiet, scared voice that wavers.

Ashton tightens his arms around my waist, hugging me from behind. "I'm sorry, angel." He whispers.

I choke back a sob. Mummy and Daddy are really gone. They aren't ever going to come and find me. They broke their promise to me.

I burst into tears, turning around to sit in Aston's lap with my chest against his. I put my arms around his neck and shove my face into the crook of his neck.

Ashton wraps his arms around my waist. He rests his head against the side of mine, burying his face in my messy hair. It got messy while I slept. He makes soft cooing noises at me, trying to calm me down but it doesn't really work well.

Nothing he can say with take away the gaping hole now in my chest. It feels like something is constricting my heart, like someone has plunged their giant hand in it and is squeezing as hard as they possibly can. It's like my chest is... empty. The only thing is my dead, beating heart that echoes around my chest quietly.

"Everything's going to be fine, Rosy." He whispers into my hair, rubbing my back gently.

My body shakes as I struggle to get a breath into my lungs. I cry out loudly again. "I want my Mummy and Daddy!" I sob hysterically, my words short and cut off by my tears.

"I know, angel, I know." He sighs, rubbing my back again.

I sob again, crushing my face into his neck again, my tears flooding down his skin. Why me? Why are my parents gone? Why am I ten years older than I thought I was? Why me? What did I do that was so bad that I deserve this?

I feel myself get lifted up as Ashton stands.

I cling onto him like the child I thought I was.

I hear a light get switched on, and peek out from his shoulder to see him taking me into the bathroom again. He sits me on the sink bench half facing him half facing the mirror on the wall.

"Look, Rosy. I know what you're feeling. I lost my sister and father on the same day, and neither of them deserved it. I know what you're going through." He starts quietly.

I sob again. He lost his father and sister? Like I lost my mother and father? Then he must know how empty and heartbroken I feel.

"It's hard when you lose someone close to you. You feel like someone has torn out your heart and everything inside of you has gone completely cold." He continues softly.

I nod, resting my head on his shoulder lightly, my face towards his neck as I sit half on his hip, his arms around my waist. That is exactly what I feel like.

Spot on. My cries and sobs quieten down a little bit as I listen to Ashton talking to me. I like the sound of his sweet voice; it's very calming to me.

"When I lost my sister and my father, my other sister and my mother and I were devastated." He says sadly. So he has two sisters... well one now. "But because we had each other, we were able to overcome that grief and carry on with our lives." He says to me.

I nod softly, sniffing.

"You still have your brother, don't ever forget that. When I first met Jack, he was depressed and he was bleak. He was stuck in his state of grief at losing his entire family. He thought he had lost you. Finding you has given him a ray of sunshine, I've never seen him act like he does around you. He loves you, Rosy, don't ever forget that." He says.

I make Jack happy? That is a good thing, I like making him happy. He is my big brother after all.

"You need to know that even though your parents aren't here to guide you anymore, you still have Jack. You have someone who cares about you more than anyone else. You need to find console in him, because if you do, losing your parents won't seem so hurtful." He tells me.

I nod, stronger this time. I sniff again, wiping tears off my cheeks with the back of my hand.

"And don't forget you have me, too." He whispers quietly, so quiet I can barely hear him.

That brings me up short. Just hearing him say that makes my heart do summersaults. I wonder why. But I nuzzle down closer to him anyway, happy for his comfort and attention. For some strange reason his skin is zapping me, like when you rub your feet on the carpet. It's nice though, so I don't complain.

"Look in the mirror." Ashton instructs me.

I turn my head towards it obediently, doing as he says.

"What do you see?" He asks me next.

What do I see?

I see a tiny, tiny girl with a lot of frizzy, wild blonde hair and overly big sky blue eyes that are wide and frightened. Her eyes are watery and her face blotchy from crying. She has bags under her eyes. She is clinging to a tall, handsome boy who looks fresh and neat, holding him like he is the only thing keeping her from drowning.

I see a frightened, terrified girl. I don't want to be that girl.

"Do you want to know what I see?" Ashton asks me, his voice soft and quiet. It's... nice, comforting.

I hesitate for a moment, but then nod cautiously, slowly. I want to know what he sees in the mirror. I want to know if he sees the horrible image I see. I want to know if he sees me.

Ashton meets my eyes in the mirror, warm chocolate brown into icy sky blue. "I see an absolutely gorgeous girl who has displayed more courage than I have ever seen. I see a girl who is brave enough to do anything she wants. I see someone who can hold their own, who can do what they want without much struggle. I see a girl who has people who love her. I see you." He says honestly, his gaze not wavering from mine, not even for a moment.

My heart skips a beat. "Why?"

Ashton continues to stare into my eyes. "You were out there for ten years, completely in wolf form. You managed to avoid discovery from my father for a time, then me. You hid away from the bands of rogues around here. You stayed alive and healthy out there, all by yourself." He says.

I frown in thought. Is that true? Does he really mean that?

"You are courageous, brave and beautiful. Stunning." Ashton adds on the end in a truthful voice.

Even in this messy state he thinks I'm pretty? Aw! That's sweet of him, even if he might not mean it honestly.

I drag my gaze away from his intense eyes to the floor to hide my strong blush. He is so sweet.

Resting my head back on his shoulder, my small, skinny arms still around his neck loosely, I yawn tiredly.

"Sleep if you need to. You deserve it." Ashton murmurs quietly, picking me up again and taking me back to his room. He lies me down on his bed, pulling the covers over my tiny body for me.

That is all I need to fall peacefully back asleep.

(Ashton's POV)

I brush the hair away from my angel's eyes, happy to watch her as she sleeps peacefully.

With a sigh I lean down and kiss her forehead. I tuck her in again, stroking her face with the back of my hand. I love feeling that her skin gives mine with the intense, electrifying sparks that make my body feel hotter than usual.

I sigh again, before quietly leaving the room. I shut the door behind me, not wanting anyone to disturb her.

I make my way back down to my lounge room through the maze that is known as my house. When I reach my lounge room, I call in some of my friends, including my beta, Joshua. Yes, I am the alpha for anyone who hadn't figured that out already.

"What's up, Ashton?" Joshua asks, a grin on his face like usual. Joshua, with his light brown hair and green eyes, is completely a ladies' man. But he is saving himself for his mate, who he hasn't met yet.

"The rogue attacks are becoming frequent again." I say first off.

Growls of anger ripple around the room. No one likes rogues, especially after my Dad and sister were killed by them.

Amy, my second sister who is sixteen years old, walks in with a can of coke in her hand. "Rogues?" She whispers, frowning.

My sister has the same black hair as me, but has my mother's blue eyes, whereas I have my Dad's brown eyes. Amy comes up to my side and leans into me. I put my arm over her shoulder. "Yeah, just in the last night we've had two attacks." I say grimly.

Tears fill her eyes, but she doesn't let them fall. Out of my mother and me, she took the death of our family the hardest. She and Diana were best friends, and she was a complete Daddy's girl. So without them, she took it really hard.

That is part of the reason I am so protective of her. The other part is that I am her big brother and no one hurts my baby sister. I want her to be happy.

"Who were they attacking? Rogues always have a set target." Amy asks quietly, looking around the room at the guys.

Joshua frowns. "It was that tiny blonde wolf." He says, nodding to himself.

"Tiny?" Amy repeats, confused.

"Yeah, as in smaller than a normal wolf, let alone a werewolf." Joshua says.

Amy's eyes widen. "Not even young shifters are that small!" She exclaims.

I start to get a little agitated, clenching the hand that isn't around Amy. My wolf doesn't like people talking about his mate like that.

Rosy is his, and no one else can have her.

"Well where is she?" Amy asks.

"My room." I say in a tone of voice that screams 'no-one-disturb-the-tiny-she-wolf-and-everyone-stay-away-from-my-room-or-else'.

Amy gives me a look.

I blatantly ignore her.

"So what are we going to do about the rogue attacks?" One of the other fighters, my friend Lucas, asks. Lucas is a good fighter and friend, but he is a complete player. He always has a different girl hanging off his arm, and I wouldn't be surprised if he had an STD or something.

I frown in thought. "If they are after Rosy, we have to protect her." I say firmly, narrowing my eyes a little.

"Rosy, huh?" Lucas asks, smirking to himself.

I growl threateningly. "Leave her alone, Lucas." I snarl. I so don't want Lucas trying to play my Rosy. I am the only one who can touch her.

He gives me a puzzled expression.

I narrow my eyes at him, my chest rumbling with a very low growl.

He backs off a little, leaning back with a wary expression on his face. Good.

"Back onto the topic of rogues." Joshua says, bringing everyone's attention to him. "So we believe the rogues are after Rosy. Correct?"

"Correct." I say.

"But the question is; why are they after Rosy? Why could a tiny little wolf pose such a threat that two bands of rogues went after her in one night?" Joshua asks next.

I frown a little. "I have no idea. We're going to have to ask Jack." I say.

"Ask Jack? Why?" Lucas asks.

Do I tell them Rosy is his little sister? Luckily for me, Jack decides to walk into the room.

"Ask me what now?" He asks, looking around the room.

"Rosy. She's the one the rogues are attacking." Lucas says quickly.

Jack stiffens, a small growl coming from him. "Why would they attack Rosy?" He asks.

"That's what I wanted to ask you about." I turn to him. "In private, first off." I add towards the rest of my friends.

They nod, deciding it is better not to argue with their Alpha. Everyone in my pack knows that it is a bad idea to argue with me. It usually doesn't end very well... for them.

Jack nods, sitting down gently on one of the sofas.

Slowly all my friends leave the room, chatting with each other. All thoughts about Rosy and the rogues forgotten.

Amy stays though. She sits on the sofa opposite Jack, while I lean up against the wall with my arms crossed over my chest.

"Want to explain all this to me?" She asks, directing her question at me.

Jack answers, though. "Rosy is my little sister." He says protectively.

Amy gasps. "I thought you didn't have any family!" She exclaims.

"I didn't." He says, narrowing his eyes and emphasizing the word 'didn't'. His family and his past life is a very touchy subject.

Amy leans back a little cautiously. "So where was she all this time?"

"Lost out in the forest." Jack says simply.

"For how long?!" Amy's jaw drops.

"Ten years." Jack says.

If possible, her jaw drops even more.

"What does she look like?" Amy asks curiously.

Jack opens his mouth to answer Amy, but I cut him off.

"Beautiful." I mumble, looking away from them both.

Amy's jaw drops- again. "...Ok, my brother did not just say that." She says, completely in denial.

Even Jack is looking at me shocked.

The situation becomes very awkward. I fidget uncomfortably.

"Why do you think my sister is beautiful?" Jack finally breaks the silence.

"Because she is." Is my quick answer.

God.

This is so awkward.

Chapter Seven

Ok, I'm not going to apologize for the long wait because I always seem to be uploading late :\ I don't necessarily like the wait, but I try to get it done as quick as I can for you guys :)

I just want to thank everyone for voting and comment, it really does make me smile a lot!

I think this one is kinda shorter than the others ones, but I don't know... o.O

Enjoy!

xox

Recap:

(Ashton's POV)

"Beautiful." I mumble, looking away from them both.

Amy's jaw drops- again. "...Ok, my brother did not just say that." She says, completely in denial.

Even Jack is looking at me shocked.

The situation becomes very awkward. I fidget uncomfortably.

"Why do you think my sister is beautiful?" Jack finally breaks the silence.

"Because she is." Is my quick answer.

God.

This is so awkward.

(Rosy's POV)

With a startled little cry I bolt upright in Ashton's comfy bed. My heart is pounding so loud I can hear it, and I can feel that my eyes are wide. There is a thin sheen of sweat on my forehead.

I was having a nightmare, but I can't remember what it was about.

All I can remember was that I was in a house, and it was on fire. I can still hear the blood curdling screams of the people being burned alive from inside the home. Their screams echo all around my head, burning their sounds into my brain.

The screams sound eerily familiar, which makes it all the more real.

Tears form at the edges of my eyes as a loud, scared whimper comes from my mouth. I bring my knees up to my chest as I sit on the edge of the bed, accidentally dragging the covers onto my knees with me.

I put my forehead against my knees like I used to when I got frustrated or overwhelmed.

I hear the door get thrown open then slam shut right before something warm wraps around my tiny body. Something warm cocoons around me, making me feel very boxed in but in a nice, comforting way.

The same sparks I felt before are back, which makes me believe that it is Ashton holding me again. I had felt them last time he comforted me, but I just ignored them. They are stronger now, though.

I turn my face into his chest, crying. I don't like the sound of people screaming stuck in my head. I don't like seeing raging fires every time I close my eyes. It's horrible.

"It's alright, Rosy. Shh..." His breath washes into my ear, his voice quiet and comforting.

I whimper, a frightened sound.

He sighs. "Want to talk about it?" He offers.

I shake my head, crushing my face into his chest. His addictive scent, a fresh forest-like scent, fills my nose and clouds my mind. He smells nice, I decide.

With a frustrated sigh, I nuzzle my face into the crook of his neck. He has this aura of comfort around him, making me feel at ease with him.

I feel him breathing on my neck softly as his head finds its way through my hair to rest on my shoulder. He hugs me tighter.

A soft click signals someone opening the closed bedroom door. My eyes peek up over Ashton's broad shoulder. I am met by Jack's confused look. I frown a little. Is he still upset at me?

As if sensing I was anxious about him, Jack smiles at me weakly. He sits on the bed behind Ashton. I fidget a little in Ashton's arms, bringing my hand up over Ashton's shoulder to reach out for him. Jack smiles weakly again, and holds my hand.

With a content little sigh I settle back down into Ashton's embrace and close my eyes. In a moment, I fall asleep again.

(Ashton's POV)

Rosy sighs, a cute little content noise, and settles down into my arms again. Her head rests on my shoulder, her hair tumbling down her back in blonde, curly tousles.

I am aware that Jack is behind me and that she reached out to hold his hand, and although my wolf growled at that I ignored him. She needs her brother. She needs his comfort.

When tiny little sleeping noises come from Rosy, I relax a little.

"Why does she sleep so much?" I ask quietly, the question just randomly springing to my mind.

"She has the mind of a six year old. Little kids love to sleep, and need to because they use up a lot of their energy." Jack answers back just as quietly. "And although her body and appearance may be that of a sixteen year old, her mind if still young. It needs to rest."

I nod. That kind of makes sense.

"Plus the fact that she just forced her body to shift while being stuck in wolf form for ten years, then having to go through the emotional trauma of realising she's ten years older than she thought she was and facing the fact that her parents died." He says.

I frown a little. "When are you going to tell her that her parents didn't actually 'die'?" I ask.

Now Jack frowns. "When she matures a little. I don't want to tell her right now that her parents were kil- murdered." He corrects himself quietly.

Even after ten years, Jack still isn't comfortable with the subject of his parent's passing.

You see, I was eight when Jack stumbled onto my dad's territory. He was bruised and covered in blood- blood that wasn't his own might I add. When he explained that his family have been massacred, my Mum and Dad took him in and raised him.

Jack went on to become the pack's best doctor, which is why I had asked him to check out Rosy. I had no idea that she would be his supposed-to-be-dead sister.

"Wait." I say suddenly. "You said Rosy has the mind of a six year old?" I ask, my voice obviously disappointed.

I can't be with a mate with the mind of a six year old. A six year old can't run a pack.

"Yes, at the moment." Jack answers cautiously.

"At the moment?" A spark of hope lights.

"Well, that's what I think. The traumatic experience she went through sort of froze her state of mind as it was. If we can teach her how to act her age, literally, then she will become a sixteen year old and age that way from then onwards." Jack explains.

I nod, trying to hide my excited smile.

"Can I ask you something, Alpha?" Jack asks hesitantly.

"Yeah, what?" I get pulled out of my day-dreams of the future, all of which include me and my Rosy.

"Is..." Jack hesitates. "Is Rosy your mate?" He asks.

I stiffen, but keep a causal face. Without hesitation I answer. "Yes."

Jack reels back in shock at my blunt answer. "W-what?"

"Rosy is my mate." I repeat calmly, feeling a proud sensation well up in my chest.

Jack leans back, letting out a long breath. "Well I guess I can't really do anything about that." He says after a while, frowning. "Just don't hurt her, yeah? Cause then I would have to do something about that." He says seriously, getting a scary look on his face. I haven't seen him like this before. He's really protective of his sister.

My wolf doesn't like being threatened. My eyes narrow. "Why would I ever hurt her?" I growl.

Jack nods, getting the message. "As long as she's happy I'm happy." He says warily, looking tired.

"Hey, Jack? What's her full name?" I ask curiously.

Jack smiles. "She has such a pretty name, she always has." He smiles at a memory.

I lean forwards, waiting for his answer in anticipation. "Well what is it?" I ask impatiently.

Jack smiles. "Rosalina."

Chapter Eight

So so so so sorry about the really long wait! I had no time to right, because the computer was being hogged by my brother... and then it was my birthday on Friday, so I didn't really do much. And then my new iPod hogged my attention, so I barely got anything done...

Anyway..

Enjoy!!

xox

Recap:

(Ashton's POV)

My wolf doesn't like being threatened. My eyes narrow. "Why would I ever hurt her?" I growl.

Jack nods, getting the message. "As long as she's happy I'm happy." He says warily, looking tired.

"Hey, Jack? What's her full name?" I ask curiously.

Jack smiles. "She has such a pretty name, she always has." He smiles at a memory.

I lean forwards, waiting for his answer in anticipation. "Well what is it?" I ask impatiently.

Jack smiles. "Rosalina."

(Rosy's POV)

I wake up and yawn. I don't know the time, but I feel better.

Pushing the covers off my feet, I slip my legs off the edge of the bed and stand up. I wobble a lot, since I haven't walked on two legs in... Ten... years.

I stumble over to the wall, leaning up against it for support. Slowly, I move my way along the wall. My feet don't do what I want. It's strange, only having two legs support you instead of four. My arms are shorter than my legs too, which is strange. But in human form I have shorter arms, that's how humans are.

When I make it to the bathroom, I take one shaky hand off the wall to open the door. It swings open, almost making me fall over. I scowl at it.

Awkwardly walking into the en suite, I use the toilet and wash my hands. I splash water on my face, which is hard because my legs are shaking a lot.

Gripping onto the edge of the sink, I look at my reflection.

My blonde hair is messy from sleeping and very tangled. It has lots of different colours in it, but is more blonde than anything else. It is kind of frizzy and curly. Mummy always told me I have nice hair.

My eyes look very big on my face, and are very bright and alert. They are an icy blue colour, like the sky on a sunny day.

My face is heart shaped. My cheeks are red as if I was wearing some of Mummy's make-up. My lips are pink.

I don't think I look very pretty.

I look skinny and wild.

I don't like looking skinny and wild.

Stumbling back out of the bathroom, I fall onto the bed heavily. My legs are hurting. It feels like I've run a marathon.

A little frustrated noise comes from me. I don't like being not able to run around. It's kind of boring, actually.

Someone knocks on the door. My head whips up as I see Ashton and Jack walk in.

I frown a little. "Why did you knock to come into your own room?" I ask Ashton, confused.

Jack chuckles at my obliviousness. "It's polite to knock when someone is in a room by themselves, Rosy." He explains.

"But it's his room." I argue, blinking a few times.

Ashton watches with amusement in his eyes.

"Yes, but you were in it by yourself. What if you were asleep or getting changed and someone just barged in without knocking?" Jack asks, his voice calm and not mean.

I think about it. "I guess that's true." I nod once.

Jack smiles at me. "Are you hungry?" He asks.

I think about it, but nod almost straight away. I haven't eaten in ages.

"Come on then." He beckons me out of the room, before leaving and heading down the hallway.

I sigh, not wanting to walk again just yet.

Standing up without a wall is hard. I wobble a bit, concentrating hard. I take a wobbly step forwards, but trip over my own feet and fall.

"Ow!" I cry, holding my sore ankle.

In less than a second Ashton is crouching down next to me. "Are you alright?" he asks, worried.

"I can't walk!" I complain, looking up at him with a frustrated glower.

Ashton sighs. His arms find their way around my waist and under my thighs. He picks me up and holds me on his hip like a little kid. My legs are on either side of him.

I rest my head on his shoulder.

Ashton carries me out of his room and down the hallway. He winds his way through his house and down a flight of stairs.

"How do you know your way around?" I ask curiously.

He chuckles. "I live here, I've always lived here." He explains.

"Oh."

Ashton walks down the stairs, still carrying me.

"Does your family live here too?"

"Yes. My sister and my Mother live here with me." He replies.

"You have a sister?" I ask excitedly.

Ashton chuckles again. "Yes."

"How old is she? Can I meet her?"

"She's sixteen, like you. You can meet her if you want, after you eat something and talk with Jack." Ashton says.

I nod, frowning a little. I am sixteen, I remind myself. "Do you know when my birthday is? I forgot." I ask him.

"No, I don't know when you're birthday is. We can ask Jack, though." He says.

I nod. "You're going to be my friend, right? Jack had lots of friends."

Ashton laughs quietly. "Yes. I'm going to be your friend."

I grin. "Cool."

We arrive in the kitchen where Jack is making me something to eat.

He turns and looks at me, before giving me a disapproving look. "Did you make Ashton carry you down here?" He asks disbelievingly.

"No!" I cry, defending myself.

Jack gives me another disbelieving look. "Rosalina." He warns.

That's my name, I think to myself.

"I didn't, really!" I say. "I fell over and he was helping me." I protest. "Right?" I ask, turning to Ashton with a pleading look in my eye.

Ashton nods. "She's right. I was just helping." He says the last four words separately, giving Jack a hard look.

Jack leans away from Ashton a bit, looking wary.

"Told you." I smirk at Jack.

His gaze turns to me, before a happy smile spreads across his face. "Still hungry?" he asks.

I nod. "Yep. What are you making?" I ask.

"I am making bacon and eggs." He says.

My eyes light up. "Really?"

Jack smiles, nodding.

"Thank you!" I cry, smiling happily.

"You're welcome." He grins back. "Why don't you go sit in the lounge room with Ashton and see if there is anything on T.V?" He suggests.

I nod. "Can I ask you something?"

"Yeah, what is it?"

"When is my birthday?" I ask.

Jack smiles to himself. "In a week or two, actually. You're almost seventeen." He says.

I nod. "Alright."

Ashton hoists me up higher on his hip.

"Let's go watch T.V." I suggest.

"Ok." He smiles at me, a dazzling smile. Again my heart flutters a tiny bit.

My hand clenches at the back of Ashton's neck in his shirt, a natural thing. He carries me to the lounge room.

I look around in awe at the spotless furniture and beautiful decor.

My mouth hangs open a little, my wide eyes wider. "I didn't know T.V's got that big." I finally say, looking at the big T.V hanging on the wall. It's black and glossy, very thin too.

Ashton chuckles. "My pack is rich."

"You're the alpha?"

He nods. "Yes, I took over when my Father passed away." He says.

"Oh... sorry."

"What for?" He asks, sounding confused.

"Bringing up someone who has passed away. Mummy said it is polite to say sorry when you do that."

"It's fine." He smiles at me.

I nod once.

Ashton puts me on the armchair and switches the T.V on. He sits on the other sofa.

"Can I put my feet up on the chair?" I ask Ashton.

He nods.

I smile to myself and curl up on the chair. Tom and Jerry area running around on the screen, enthralling me straight away. My eyes pretty much glue themselves to the T.V. I always loved this cartoon.

Five minutes later, Jack calls me in to eat.

"Food's ready, Rosy!" He calls.

I jump up and dart into the kitchen faster than I thought I could move. It hurts my legs a lot to do that, and I almost fall over face first into the kitchen bench. I whimper as my feet bump into the ground painfully. I guess I am really hungry. Sitting at the bench, Jack slides a plate of food towards me. My eyes light up.

"Thanks." I grin as he hands me a knife and fork.

"You're welcome." Jack smiles, sitting down across from me and eating his food.

Ashton comes in and eats as well.

When I finish, Jack puts my dish in the sink, feeling fuller and not hungry anymore.

"What are we going to do today?" I ask Jack, sitting down again.

"Actually, I was thinking of getting Ashton to tutor you, so you can catch up and eventually start attending high school." Jack says.

I cock my head to the side a little, my brow furrowing in confusion.

Ashton chokes on the water he was drinking. "What?"

Jack gives him a hard look. "Well if you don't want to stay here all day with Rosy and practically watch her grow up than I can do it. Maybe even get a proper tutor."

At the Ashton's eyes seem to light up. "No, no, I'll do it." He says, smiling a little to himself.

I cock my head to the side a little, clearly confused. "Huh?"

Jack's eyes flick over to me. "Nothing, Rosy. Don't worry about it." He smiles.

I shrug. "Can we start now?" I ask, my eyes lighting up. I used to love going to school and playing with my friends.

Jack chuckles. "No, Rosy. It's the weekend; no one has to learn on the weekend. It's a time to relax and have fun." Jack explains.

I pout a little, but nod anyway. "I guess you're right..."

"But," Ashton pipes up, making my gaze swing towards him, "That means we can have fun all today." He grins at me.

I grin back.

Later that morning, Jack, Ashton and I were sitting in the lounge room watching cartoons.

"What are we going to do today?" I ask, moving to lie down with my head in Jack's lap and my feet in Ashton's. Neither of them seems to mind all too much, since they aren't complaining.

Jack starts running his fingers through my tangled hair. "Well," He starts, "You need some new clothes. Maybe we could go shopping?" he suggests.

I nod absentmindedly.

"Maybe Amy could come with us." Ashton says.

"Who's Amy?" I ask, my nose wrinkling in confusion a little.

"Amy's my sister."

"Oh." I say, nodding once. "Can she come?"

"Do you want me to ask her?" Ashton asks.

"Yes." I say, adding "Please." When Jack gives me a look.

Ashton nods. For a moment he is quiet, his face blank. Then he says, "She's coming down now." He says.

I frown, sitting up to look at him without moving my feet. "How do you know that?" I ask.

Ashton taps his temple. "Mind-link. I'm the Alpha of this pack, I can communicate through minds." He says.

"Oh... right."

A minute or so later the sound of bounding feet come pounding down the stairs.

I lie back down on the sofa, my head in Jack's lap again. I stare at the ceiling, thinking to myself. What if she doesn't like me? What if she's mean to me or I make her mad?

"Ashton?" I hear a feminine voice call.

"In the lounge room, Amy." Ashton calls back, watching my face with amusement in his warm, chocolate brown eyes.

My heart beat increases the tiniest bit. Is she going to like me?

A girl with black hair like Ashton's and dark blue eyes walks in the room. She has a smile on her face.

I tense up a little bit, squishing closer to the back of the lounge in a weak attempt to cover myself. Jack brushes the hair away from my face softly. Ashton gently rubs my ankles. I'm not wearing any shoes because I don't have any yet.

"Over here, Amy." Ashton says, giving me a reassuring smile.

I bury my face in the space between Jack's arm and chest, hiding there. His body shakes with silent chuckles, making my face redden.

I feel Amy's gaze fall on me as she stands behind the sofa. I squeeze my eyes shut, my heart pounding in nervousness.

But curiosity wins over.

I peek out from behind Jack's arm, opening one wide eye.

I come face to face with Amy peering at me, making me jump back a little. My heart starts beating ever faster.

"Amy, not so close. You're scaring her." Ashton says, half growling, his voice low and protective.

Amy leans back a little bit. "She's so cute!" She says, still smiling.

I cock my head to the side a little. Does that mean she likes me? Is she going to be my friend?

"Awww!" Amy says when I tilt my head. "What's your name, hun?"

I sit up a little, still clutching Jack's arm. "Rosy."

"Well, I'm Amy. Is Rosy short for anything?" She asks curiously, leaning her elbows on the back of the sofa.

I sit up straighter, crossing my legs. "Um..." I say unsurely. I can't remember what my full name was! What do I say?!

I throw Jack a helpless look.

"Rosalina." Jack says to Amy.

I nod. That's it! I have got to remember that.

"Well isn't that a pretty name!" Amy exclaims.

Another blush makes its way to my cheeks. "Uh, thanks." I say, unsure of what to reply.

Amy grins.

I try to think of something to say to her. Come up with nothing.

Ashton leans across the sofa and puts his mouth near my ear. "Why don't you ask her if she wants to come shopping?" He whispers, his breath almost making me shiver.

My eyes widen. Yeah, I can do that!

"Thanks." I say, kind of breathlessly, to Ashton, blushing a little when he chuckles. He leans back and just goes back to watching me curiously.

I turn to Amy. "Do you want to come shopping with us?" I ask hopefully.

Her eyes light up. "I love shopping! Let's go already!" She cries. "But you have to find some new clothes first." She adds, looking at the clothes that don't fit me too well.

I blush yet again, but nod.

Amy sucks in a breath as an idea pops into her mind. "You can wear some of my old clothes! They are too small for me, but they might fit you!" She says happily.

My eyes light up. "Really?" I ask excitedly.

"Yeah, come on!" She exclaims, grabbing onto my wrist.

I clamber over the back of the lounge, which I probably shouldn't do, and race after Amy as we run back up the stairs.

Amy shows me her room, which is just down the hallway from Ashton's. I'm going to get lost sooner or later...

Amy's room is big, to say the least. It's very purple and green coloured, too.

"Go sit on my bed and I will see if I can find something small for you to wear. You're so skinny and short." She observes.

"Yeah..." I mumble, moving to jump onto her bed. I guess I am really small compared to most people, excluding ten year olds.

Amy opens her wardrobe and starts rummaging around for something for me to wear. When she pops her head back out, she has an armful of clothes ready for me.

"Here, go try these on." She encourages, nudging me towards her bathroom.

"Why does every room have a separate bathroom?" I ask quietly.

She chuckles. "Not every room. Just mine and Ashton's." She tells me.

"Oh. Ok."

I walk in the big bathroom and pull on the clothes she gave me. Besides for the bra and underclothes, which fit nicely, the rest of the clothes fit perfectly too.

It's a tight white singlet with a half-length light blue denim jacket over the top. Denim shorts that aren't too short but don't end anywhere near my knees. Everything fits nicely.

"Are you ready yet?" I hear Amy call from outside the door.

I take a look in the mirror. I look nice, though my long hair is still messy. "Yes." I answer her, nodding to myself.

She comes in and gasps.

"What? Is something wrong?" I ask, frowning a little. I thought I looked nice...

"You look so hot!" She exclaims suddenly.

A bright red blush colours my cheeks again. "Um, thanks." I think.

"Come on, I think I have the perfect shoes for you!" She says excitedly, grabbing my wrist again and dragging me back into her room.

She sits me down on a chair in front of a make-up mirror.

Amy disappears in her closet for something, and then reappears a moment later with a shoe box in her hand.

"Because you're so tiny, I have to give you some of my old stuff that doesn't fit anymore." She explains, sitting down in front of me.

She opens the box and pulls out a pair of really strappy, white, flat sandals.

"Most people just keel these Gladiator Sandals, because they look like what the Gladiators used to wear." She explains.

"What's a Gla-Gladi...?" I try pronouncing the word, but the letters get all jumbled up.

"A Gladiator?"

"Yeah, that."

"A Gladiator is a figure from history. Gladiators are what the people are called who used to fight each other or animals in a big stadium." She tells me.

"Ok." I shrug, watching her as she slips the shoes onto my dirty feet.

"There." She says, sitting back.

"I like them." I say, grinning to myself.

Amy grins. "Yeah, they look nice on you."

"It feels weird wearing shoes." I say as Amy turns me back towards the mirror.

"Don't worry, you'll get used to it." She says as she starts brushing my hair. "You're hair is really long." She says, kind of shocked.

I shrug. It does almost reach my bum, I think to myself.

In a few fluid motions, Amy has tied my hair up in a high pony tail, leaving out my fringe.

I look at myself and smile. I look nicer like this.

Amy watches me carefully, smiling when I smile. "I think the guys are going to like this new look, especially Ashton." She says, grinning.

For the hundredth time today I blush, kind of confused, though. What is that supposed to mean? I shrug it off casually, forgetting about it.

"Ready to go?" She says.

I grin. "Yeah."

"But first we gotta get past the boys without a hitch." She says.

I groan.

Chapter Nine

Happy easter for a few days ago!! I was going to upload, but I wanted to upload all of my stories at once and the other chapters weren't finished...

Anyway, hope you enjoy the holidays/long weekend! I know i am ;)

Enjoy!

xox

Recap:

I look at myself and smile. I look nicer like this.

Amy watches me carefully, smiling when I smile. "I think the guys are going to like this new look, especially Ashton." She says, grinning.

For the hundredth time today I blush, kind of confused, though. What is that supposed to mean? I shrug it off casually, forgetting about it.

"Ready to go?" She says.

I grin. "Yeah."

"But first we gotta get past the boys without a hitch." She says.

I groan.

"Come on, we might as well get this over with." Amy giggles, prancing out of the room.

I follow her, not wanting to get lost in Ashton's big house. We walk down the stairs and back to the lounge room.

As soon as we walk back in, Jack's and Ashton's eyes fall on me, both lighting up happily.

I blush and hedge behind Amy self-consciously.

She laughs at my embarrassment. "Aw, isn't she adorable?" Amy coos, pinching my cheek. I slap her hand away lightly.

I swear I see Ashton's smile grow wider and warmer, but I can't be sure because Jack distracts me by talking.

"You look nice, Rosy. Ready to go?" He asks me.

I nod enthusiastically. "Yes!"

"Well let's go then." He smiles proudly.

The four of us head out to Ashton's car.

"Ashton, can you drive?" I ask curiously.

I feel his breath on my neck as he talks from behind me. He chuckles. "Yes Rosy."

"What about you, Jack?" I ask.

He is walking in front of me. He chuckles too. "Yes, I can drive Rosy."

"Oh. Ok. So who's going to drive?" I ask next.

"I am." Ashton says straight away.

"Ok."

When we arrive at the shopping mall, I start to feel a little intimidated by the amount of people here. There are so many smells, so many bright colours, and so many stores. It's all a little to suffocating for me. I start to feel claustrophobic.

"Whoa..." Is all I can force out of my suddenly tight throat. I shrink down in my seat a little.

Ashton and Jack get out of the car as soon as it stops, soon followed by an overly excited Amy. I never knew a girl could get so excited over a simple shopping trip.

Ashton opens my door. "Come on, Rosy." He throws me a reassuring smile.

I gulp, but nod anyway. Unclipping my seatbelt, I hesitantly hop out of the car and stand next to Ashton. Everything seems bigger and brighter when in out of the car.

"Ready to go?" He smiles his dazzling smile at me.

I smile back weakly, still feeling kind of overwhelmed. There are just so many people here...

Amy leads us in, walking around like she owns the place. I follow her like a lost little puppy. Both the boys trail behind us, talking amongst themselves but keeping an eye on us.

Amy squeals all of a sudden and grabs my arm. "Come on, let's go here!" She exclaims, dragging me towards a clothes store. I hurriedly twist my body so I don't smash into anyone.

"Isn't this pretty?" She sighs, pointing out a shirt.

I nod. It is nice...

"Come on, let's go try stuff on." She says happily, pulling clothes of random racks and putting them in my arms.

When we eventually leave the store, I have two bags full of t-shirts, dresses and a few scarves. I was a bit worried about the price, but Amy says that I need clothes and money is no object for them. She said as long as she knows how to use it she can spend it.

The guys look at me with amused expressions, waiting patiently outside the store.

I shrug, blushing a little and looking away from them, kind of embarrassed.

Amy doesn't seem fazed, though. She loves this way too much. "Where to next?" She asks herself quietly, getting strange looks from everyone.

I follow after her, not wanting to get lost.

I can just tell that this is going to be a long day.

By the time we stop for lunch, my feet are killing me. I'm only carrying five or six filled up bags, but it still gets tiring. I didn't think clothes could be this heavy.

Amy leads us to a table, looking comfortable. "Just wait here while the three of us go get food, ok Rosy?" Amy says, putting the bags on one of the tables in the food court.

I grunt lazily and flop down on the sofa-like seat that runs around the inside of the perimeter of the food court.

Ashton chuckles at me quietly.

I watch as my friends and my brother all head off to get some food from one of the restaurants that are scattered everywhere.

The smell of grease and coffee start to flood my nose. Loud music and constant chatter from everyone around here fill my ears, as well as many heartbeats. I can feel the cold table underneath my palms as I lean forwards. Bright colours and lots of busy people fill my vision.

I haven't been near this many people in ten years. It's all getting to be very overpowering.

Soon enough another scent fills my nose. A sour scent, like dirty fur and blood. I know that scent all too well.

Rogue.

But only one. I think. I hope.

My eyes dart over towards where the scent is coming from. It's a bit hard to find it because of all the other smells, but I eventually find its source.

There is a group of human guys with the rogue. They are staring at me like I am something to eat. It's disgusting and is making me feel uncomfortable. I look away, hoping they forget all about me as I try to forget them.

But no such luck. A moment later, someone slides onto the seat next to me and puts their arm around my waist, a little too tightly.

I jump in fright, my heart beating a little faster. The rogues scent becomes stronger. "What are y-you doing?" I stutter, trying to lean away from him.

"Oh, nothing babe." He smirks at me, something that makes my insides crawl.

I recoil away from him, trying to squeeze out of his arms.

But he isn't having any of that. He pulls me closer, almost painfully. "Aw, don't be like that babe." He purrs, leaning closer. Too close.

I lean away again, starting to feel kind of panicked. What is he going to do to me? "G-get off me!" I cry angrily.

"You don't sound so sure there, darling." He chuckles, pulling me closer yet again so my side is pressed up against his. I don't see what's so funny.

My face crinkles up in distaste. "Please get off me." I say again, this time close to crying. I don't like being touched by this person. I don't even know him! And he is a rogue werewolf. I don't like rogues. I try not to cry.

"You look hot today, babe. We should go off and ditch our friends." He says suggestively.

"No!" I say loudly, trying to shove him off me again. It doesn't work; he's stronger than me. As he stands, dragging me with him, I start panicking even more.

A low sounding, furious growl travels through the air.

Both the rogues' head and my head snap up in the direction its coming from. I see Ashton, Amy and Jack all looking angry, but Ashton looks the angriest. His eyes aren't the soft brown I've gotten used to, but an angry dark black.

I throw him a helpless look.

The three of them walk over here casually, so they don't draw attention from the humans here. I watch them with a rising feeling of dread.

Amy and Jack slide in on the seats of the table across from me and put the food on the table normally. Ashton moves to sit next to me. I try to move closer to him, but the rogue stops me. He's still standing, and his arm is still around my waist. It's not as tight anymore, though.

"What do you think you're doing?" Ashton growls through clenched teeth. He easily detaches the rogue's arm from around my waist and pulls me to his chest. I make a small whining noise quietly and clutch onto him desperately. I bury my face in the space between his arm and chest, seeking his comfort. The warmth from his body helps calm me down.

I don't hear the rest of the conversation; I chose to block it out and focus on listening to something else. The only other thing I hear though is Ashton's heart beating, so I listen to that.

I hear growls and snarls, but I block them out too. It's a bit hard, but I manage. I don't want to hear anything anymore.

After a while I feel the presence of the rogue leave. I realise that I am shaking a little bit, out of fear or relief I don't know. Something warm rubs up and down my back reassuringly, making me feel a little more relaxed.

"Rosy?" I hear Ashton say softly.

"Yeah?" I whisper back. My voice wavers.

"Are you alright, angel?"

"Mhmm..." I mumble, not trusting my voice anymore.

He hugs me closer protectively. I clutch his shirt tighter in my closed fists.

"What was that all about?" Jack asks, growling a little threateningly.

I whimper quietly. "I was just sitting here and he came over and I could smell he was a rogue and he starting touching me and he wouldn't let go even when I told him to and even when I said please." I say really fast, kind of mumbling.

Ashton growls and tightens his arm around me.

"Rosy, we can't understand you when you mumble into Ashton's shirt. You need to come out of there and talk properly." Jack says softly.

I whimper again, and shake my head. I feel safer like this, like I have someone who can protect me because I am not strong enough to do it myself. I am still shaking a little. Rogues like that guy scare me. First it was the two attacks out in the forest, and now this. What do they want? Why are there so many of them around now?

"Rosy-" Jack starts again, sighing.

Ashton snarls, cutting him off. "She's fine like she is." He snaps.

I feel wariness pulse off Jack. "Well did you hear what she said?" Jack asks, sounding submissive.

"She said he just came over here and wouldn't stop touching her. She knew he was a rogue." Ashton says through gritted teeth, sounding possessively angry.

An annoyed little growl comes from Jack and Amy.

I clench my fists in Ashton's shirt again. It must look strange to people who may be looking at us to see me squishing so close to him and burying my head in the side of his chest, but I couldn't care any less.

"We have to be more careful from now on." Jack decides.

Ashton nods.

When we finally get home that day, we have so many shopping bags that my arms are starting to hurt from carrying them.

"Come on, Rosy. I had one of my friends do something for you while we were out." Ashton smiles at me, heading for the stairs. He has shopping bags on his arms too. He's calmed down now, and so have I. His pack knows about the rogue at the shopping centre, so there are people scouting around for him now.

I struggle to keep up with his large strides. "What?" I ask, now curious.

"It's a surprise." He smirks.

I scowl at his back as he climbs the stairs. "Can you walk a little slower, please?" I ask politely.

"Oh. Yeah, sure. Sorry." He says, slowing down a bit and allowing me to catch up.

"Where'd Amy go?" I ask next.

"She's just putting some finishing touches on your surprise."

"Oh, ok."

Ashton leads me through his house. Without him I would get so lost.

Finally I recognise the corridor we are walking down.

"That's your room, right?" I point to one of the closed doors.

He chuckles. "Yes."

"And that's Amy's?" I point to one a little further down.

He nods.

"So where's Jack's room?" I ask, frowning a little.

"That one back there." Ashton points to one we just passed by.

"Oh. Ok." I say again.

We walk past Ashton's door and stop by Amy's door.

"What are we doing here?" I frown.

"This is your surprise." He smiles down at me.

I give him a confused look, my head tilting to the side a bit.

Then, someone opens Amy's door from the inside. I look into her room, and see that is has changed around a bit. There is a new single bed next to Amy's bed with light purple covers. There is a new wardrobe against the wall and a new bedside table next to the new bed.

My eyes light up. "Is this for me?" I ask hopefully, looking back up at Ashton.

"It sure is." Amy answers at the door, smiling.

I drop the bags and throw my arms around her. "Thank you!" I cry happily.

She laughs, and pats my back once. "No problem. How about we start putting your clothes in the wardrobe?" She suggests, smiling at me.

I nod excitedly.

Amy picks up the bags I dropped and walks away to take them to my wardrobe.

I turn back to Ashton and hug him around the neck too, which is a bit hard because he is so tall. Wherever my skin touches his, the same sparks as before erupt and make me want to shiver. They are nice.

"Thank you." I say gratefully, wrapping my arms around his waist and hugging him again. Again the same sparks explode between my skin and his.

"N-no problem." He smiles his dazzling smile at me again, talking a little nervously.

I smile at him and take the bags off him.

"Hurry up, Rosy!" Amy calls at me.

"Coming!" I call back, bouncing over to her.

For a while Amy shows me how to do girly things. After hanging up the clothes she shoved me where to fold everything. She showed me where everything goes. She showed me where to put my dirty clothes after a shower.

She showed me how to tie my hair up, but I can't do it because it's so long.

"Do you like having it that long?" Amy had asked me, frowning a little bit at the end.

I had shrugged my shoulders at her. "I like it like this." I had told her, smiling a little. It was true; I do like my hair when it's this long.

Amy had showed me how to do a lot of things. Like straighten or curl my hair. How to put on make-up, though I didn't really like it. How to use a mobile phone, how to do my nails, how do lots of girly things.

"This is tiring." I complain hours later.

"No it's not! It's fun!" Amy laughs. "Now, what colour goes with pink?" She asks me, holding up a pink shirt.

I look through my clothes. "White? Yellow? Blue? Black? Lots of colours!" I guess.

She smiles. "Good. You're learning." She smiles again, laughing.

I breathe out a long sigh. "I want to go for a run." I say. I am getting bored and restless. Plus I haven't been in wolf form for ages.

"I think I'm going to stay here. Why don't you go ask Jack of Ashton if they can go with you?" She suggests.

"Ok." I smile.

Bouncing out of Amy's and mine room, I look down the hallway. Now which room was Jack's? I pad down the hallway and knock on his door.

He doesn't answer, so I open it. His room is big like Ashton's and Amy's and has a big bed. He isn't in here, so I shrug and shut the door again. I wonder where he is?

I walk back to Ashton's room.

Knocking on his door I wait to see if he is in there.

"Come in." I hear him grunt unhappily, sounding annoyed.

I open the door hesitantly. Did I make him unhappy? "Ashton? Oh, I'm sorry." I say sadly, going to shut the door behind me.

In a fraction of a second Ashton is standing in front of me, his hand holding the door and stopping it from being shut. He pulls me into his chest, his arms tight around my waist. I realise he isn't wearing a shirt. His skin is warm and makes sparks shoot down my body. My face flushes a little.

"What's wrong, angel?"

"N-nothing." I stutter. "Did I w-wake you up?" I ask, looking at his messy bed and his messy hair, trying to speak through my bright red cheeks.

He nuzzles his face into the hair on top of my head. "Not really. I couldn't sleep."

"Oh, umm... ok."

"Is there anything you wanted?" He asks.

"Oh yeah! I wanted to ask you if you maybe wanted to come for a run with me? Amy doesn't want to and I can't find Jack, and I don't really want to go by myself." I say, babbling. "And I just thought that because you are my friend you might want to come, because I am sick of doing girl stuff with Amy cause it's getting a bit boring."

Ashton chuckles, cutting me off from my talking. "I would love to come for a run with you." He smiles down at me.

My eyes brighten up. "Really? Then let's go, come on!" I cry happily, grabbing his hand and dragging him out of his room.

He laughs behind me at my eagerness.

Suddenly I stop.

Ashton bumps into me, almost sending me flying to the ground, but his hands on my hips stop me from falling. "What's wrong?" He asks, sounding worried.

I look up at him sheepishly. "I don't know where to go."

Ashton laughs. "Lucky I do, then." He smiles at me again.

Ashton starts leading me through his house until we get to his back door. "You know how to shift, right?" he asks me, turning his heads to look back at me as he leads me out by the hand.

"Um, not really." I admit. "I kinda forgot."

"All you need to do is the opposite of shifting back to human form. Imagine what it is like to be in wolf form and bring out that form." He instructs.

"Oh, and take your clothes off first. You don't want them ripping." He adds.

"Ok." I say, taking in his instructions. "Um... can I ask you a question?" I ask quietly, my voice really soft.

Ashton stops to turn and look back at me. "What is it, angel?" He asks me just as quietly, bringing one of his hands up to touch my cheek.

"You're my friend, right? I can ask you things, right?"

"Of course." He says.

"If... if my Daddy and Mummy where still here, would they be teaching me this stuff?" I ask sadly, trying not to cry.

Ashton sighs. "Yes they would be, angel." He smiles. "They would have done anything for you." He says.

"You really think that?"

"Of course. You're their daughter, no matter what."

I smile at him. "Thank you." I say softly, sounding way older than I thought I was. I put my hand on his shoulder and stand up on my toes to press a small kiss to his cheek, which is a bit hard because he is so tall.

I swear I see him blush.

Any spelling/grammer mistakes??

Chapter Ten

Ok so I know it was a long wait... but these last two weeks have been anything but peaceful for me. At least the chapter got done, right?

So I just want to ask one quick question: what do you all think of the new cover? Well, its not exactly new but this is the first time I've uploaded since I put it up. But anyway, what do you all think?

Anyway, enjoy!

xox

The next day is Sunday. I spend it 'hanging out' with Amy and Ashton. That's what Amy calls it anyway.

I am sitting on a sofa with my legs down it, leaning against Ashton's side. He is sitting straight, looking at their impossibly large T.V. His arm is over my shoulder and down across my chest, playing with the ends of my hair loosely. His eyes are glued to the T.V, watching whatever show is on.

Amy is sitting on the armchair, watching the show too.

I'm not watching the show. I don't even know what it is about. All I know is that there are a lot of singers on it. I am too busy thinking about random things. Like how I am starting school with Ashton tomorrow. Where Jack is. What else Amy is going to teach me about being a sixteen year old girl.

I look up as Jack and a pretty girl walk in the room.

"Hi guys." Jack smiles. "This is Mandy. She's my mate." He says proudly with a bright, big smile.

I take another look at Mandy. Brown hair and bright brown eyes. Thin but not too thin. A nice smile.

A happy grin curls up my lips. "Hi! I'm Rosy." I say over excitedly.

"You must be Jack's sister. It's nice to meet you. Aren't you a pretty thing?" She coos at me, smiling warmly.

I blush. I beckon Jack over. He leaves Mandy's side to come near me. I lean up to his ear. "I like her. She's pretty." I say happily.

He chuckles. "I like her too."

For a while we all get to know Mandy. She's really nice and seems to like Jack a lot. She knows that I was lost for ten years and I still have the mind of a six year old, and accepts that I am a little childish at times.

I yawn a little. It's getting late.

"Come on Rosy, bed time." Ashton tells me.

I make a little annoyed noise. "I'm not tired though!" I complain tiredly.

He chuckles. "Yes you are. Arms up." He instructs, standing up.

I lift my arms up, wondering why. Ashton picks me up and puts his hands under my thighs. I wrap my legs around his waist and rest my head on his shoulder tiredly. I yawn again and close my eyes.

"Say goodnight." Ashton tells me.

"Good... night." I yawn in the middle again, not knowing who I am talking to.

I hear chuckles as Ashton carries me up the stairs. He takes me to Amy's room and tucks me into bed. Kissing my forehead, he says goodnight to me and I say it back, before peacefully falling back asleep.

~Rosy's Dream~

I am six now. Not sixteen. Six.

It's dark, and I am alone in the forest. Mummy and Daddy said we are playing the silence game. They ran off in wolf form, but I don't like being alone.

So I followed them.

When I catch up I see them in a small clearing, facing down three big men.

"Mummy? Daddy?" I cry, looking at their bloody wounds.

Everyone's head turn to me as I crouch down, almost crying.

Mummy shifts back. "Rosy, darling, go back where we left you. We'll be there soon." She tries to coax me away.

I shake my head. "No! I want to stay with you!" I start crying.

"Listen to your Mum, kid. Go away." One of the men growls at me.

I cry harder.

"Go on sweetheart. We'll be there soon. We love you." Mummy says.

I sniff. "Promise?"

"We promise darling." Mummy smiles weakly.

I turn and dart away, but I trip over a root and end up falling. My ankle starts hurting.

Growls erupt from behind me. I hear two loud bangs and howls of pain.

"Mummy? Daddy?" I cry, stumbling back to the clearing. When I get there I scream. Blood is everywhere. I see two lumps of fur, not moving. Two wolves. I scream again.

"Looks like they broke their promise, kid." One of the men sneer. I see he has a gun.

"Daddy!" I scream, running for him. I tangle my fingers in his fur and shake him. He doesn't move. Neither does Mummy. "No!" I scream, crying again.

They aren't even breathing.

~End of Dream~

I wake up with a startled yelp. Something warm slips down my face. Tears. I am crying my eyes out silently. My heart is pounding out of control.

Every dark shadow is scaring me.

I start hyperventilating.

"A-Amy!" I stutter, still crying and freaking out.

She stirs. "Just go back to sleep, Rosy." She mumbles, rolling over and going back to sleep.

I whimper.

Trying to sleep isn't going to help me. I am too scared.

I stand up and leave the room, ignoring my shaking limbs.

I look down the hallway, checking to see is anyone is there. I'm still crying, blinking hastily to clear my vision. I walk down the dark hallway to Jack's room. I feel like he is the one I need comfort from, because he is my family after all.

Opening the door, I see he is asleep with Mandy. They look happy.

I stand at the end of the bed. "J-Jack?" I cry, my heart still pounding. It's really dark, it's only early morning. The sun isn't up quite just yet.

Mandy bolts up out of the bed and screams in shock. I stumble backwards, frightened out of my skin. My eyes go wide as I feel my pupils dilate a bit.

Jack bolts upright, his eyes dark with anger, and his growls deep threatening sound. His eyes search for danger until they land on me.

I whimper, still crying.

"What the hell, Rosy?" He yells at me. "You can't just come into someone's room in the middle of the night! We were trying to sleep!"

I flinch away from him.

I hear Ashton and Amy jolt awake and exit their bedrooms into the hallway.

"Don't you know how to act normal, Rosy? Why did you just walk in here?!" He screams at me, getting louder, standing up. I can see his eyes are dark.

My heart goes into overdrive as fresh tears flow down my face. Why is he yelling at me? What did I do wrong?

Mandy rushes to his side. "Calm down, Jack. Can't you see she's scared?"

Jack calms down in an instant. He looks at me. "Shit. Rosy I'm-"

I cut him off by letting out a loud sob as I finally break down. I turn and bolt from it, right past a murderous looking Ashton and frightened Amy.

I bolt right down the stairs.

"Rosy, Rosy wait!" I hear Jack call after me.

I cry louder, seeing my parent's dead bodies flash behind my eyes. Two lumps of fur, covered in blood and not moving. They're not even breathing. I use my nose to guide me to the scent of the forest, wanting to run and just run forever.

When I exit Ashton's house, I leap off the back porch and shift in mid air, my clothes ripping right off my body.

Don't you know how to be normal, Rosy?

Jack's accusing words hit me like a tonne of bricks.

I bolt for the forest, still crying.

Even in wolf form. It's quite uncomfortable.

I hear someone race after me. I continue running anyway, not knowing where I am going. My heart is still in over drive, and I feel like it is going to explode. It makes my chest constrict painfully, making it hard to breathe.

I run right through a river, and then turn down wind. That way no one can follow me and my scent is erased.

I run, and I run, and I run.

I don't know how long I run for. I run until the sun is just starting to shine on the world and the birds are just stirring.

I am still crying. Fear is the only thing I am feeling besides for panic. Every dark shadow threatens to hold something that will jump out at me, wielding a gun. Every bush could be a mound of fur that isn't moving. Everything is scaring me.

I run until the birds start waking up and the sun is just peeking up over the horizon. I run for what seems like hours to me.

When I hear voices, I slow down cautiously, my eyes wide and my ears high.

"Why are we out here at the crack of dawn again?" Someone yawns.

Someone else sighs. "We are out studying the birds. We need to know what time each species wakes up."

The voices get closer.

I continue running, feeling more frightened before. I burst through a cluster of bushes and stumble onto a hiking track.

I am greeted by two shocked faces.

"Whoa, a wolf!" The younger man exclaims.

I whimper in fright, backing away from them. My ear flick back a little as my eyes dart around. I can't hear anyone but the two humans and I can't see much either.

"Hey, no don't go away!" The younger one says, and excited look crossing his face.

I whine and back away faster, preparing to turn and leg it out of there.

"No, careful-" The other man says before I yelp and trip down something hard.

I tumble nose over tail down a steep hill, yelping and whimpering in pain. My back hits something hard and I cough painfully. When I finally tumble to a stop I slip down something damp. My hind legs and thighs get caught under a thick, heavy log that presses against my back.

I yowl in pain as the log crushes the bottom half of my body.

Leaves and twigs stick to every part of my body. There is a gash down my back staining the blonde of my fur bright red.

I whimper loudly again, trying to wiggle my way out. It only makes it hurt worse. I feel my bones creak and ache more.

The two males scramble down the hill, knocking more leaves and dirt onto me. I turn my head, closing my eyes to shield them from the debris.

I howl in pain, trying to get out of the tight spot I am in. But I don't howl for Jack or for my family this time. No. I howl for Ashton.

I howl and I howl and I howl, until my howls for help turn to howls of immense pain.

The males cover their ears from the noises I make.

"Damn she has a set of lungs on her!" One exclaims.

"Just get the log off her!" The older one yells back.

The two starts pushing the log, but it doesn't move an inch. It's way too heavy for the both of them.

Am I going to be stuck here forever?

"She's just a baby! How'd she get stuck in there?" One says.

"Look at her teeth! She' not a baby! She's old enough to be on her own!" The older one grunts, pushing against the log again.

I howl once more, pleading for Ashton to come.

A ferocious growl comes from behind me as I hear a set of paws pound this way. I howl, quieter this time.

Ashton pounds closer, snarling. He leaps over the log effortlessly, making the humans scatter with frightened looks on their faces.

Ashton whines at me quietly, pawing at my shoulder. I whimper at him, feel the bottom half of my body start to go numb.

An infuriated growl comes from his black wolf as his eyes go darker than I've ever seen them before. He pushes at the log with his front paws, using all his strength, making it shift right off me and continue rolling down the hill.

I let out a great bark of relief.

Ashton leans over me and picks me up by the ruff of my neck and takes me out of the hole I was stuck in. I practically scream out in pain as my back stretches.

Ashton whimpers and sets me on the ground gently. He leans down and starts licking the fur on my back in an attempt to help me.

The older human shuffles closer and reaches out to touch me.

Ashton growls at me, hovering over me protectively.

"I'm not gonna hurt her." He says softly, touching my back. I flinch. Ashton growls.

"What are you doing?" The younger one asks as the older one picks me up, ignoring Ashton's snarls and barks.

"She needs veterinary care." The older one simply says.

"What about him?" He asks, looking at Ashton warily.

"He can do what he wants. I wouldn't be able to stop him anyway."

The man carries me back up the slope, Ashton following right behind him, growling still. I keep making whining and whimpering softly. Ashton licks my paw lightly.

He walks down the trail and we arrive at an empty parking lot. There is a Ute parked there.

"We can't just take a wolf to the vet!" The younger man hisses.

"The vet clinic near the forest is closed this week. We can take her there and let her rest." The older one says simply, glaring at the younger one.

I get put in the back of the Ute. He clips a collar around my neck, much to my protest.

Ashton jumps up into the Ute with me. He lies down around me, forming a protective barrier around me.

The car starts and we are off. I wonder what Ashton thinks of this. He probably thinks that I'm a little baby who ran for no reason. He's probably angry at me, like Jack. But why would he come if he was angry?

"Is he her Dad or something?" I listen as the younger human asks a question.

"Obviously not." The older one replies, "Look at her. She's completely blonde coloured besides for that ear. He's completely black. Not even their eye colours are the same. Of course he's not her Father."

Ashton growls impatiently. I whimper at him, pawing at his leg as much as I can. Ashton looks down at me and makes a whining noise in the back of his throat. He nuzzles his face into the side of my head. He rests his head on the back of my neck gently.

My back and hind legs are making me feel uncomfortable, because they are aching as if they are bruised.

Ashton licks my head softly, and whines.

I still feel frightened. That... nightmare... was just horrible. It's scaring me.

Somewhere in the back of my mind I realise that I am shaking a lot.

Something doesn't feel right about this and that dream.

Chapter Eleven

Sorry about the long wait, I am quite busy with all the tests I'm having at school :\ But at least the chapter's here! I'm not quite sure I like this one... In fact, I don't think I like it at all. But I can't be bothered to change it, so eh...

Thanks for all the comments and votes I've been getting, and for the fans too :) Makes me happy that people like what I'm writing :)

Oh, and just a warning, there are quite a few POV changes in this one... hehe, sorry :)

Enjoy!

xox

Recap:

Ashton growls impatiently. I whimper at him, pawing at his leg as much as I can. Ashton looks down at me and makes a whining noise in the back of his throat. He nuzzles his face into the side of my head. He rests his head on the back of my neck gently.

My back and hind legs are making me feel uncomfortable, because they are aching as if they are bruised.

Ashton licks my head softly, and whines.

I still feel frightened. That... nightmare... was just horrible. It's scaring me.

Somewhere in the back of my mind I realise that I am shaking a lot.

Something doesn't feel right about this and that dream.

The two humans start the Ute and drive off.

I start to wish I had mind-link with Ashton so I could talk with him. But I can only have that if I am in his pack.

Barely ten minutes later the car stops and the humans hop out. The older one comes around to the side where I am collared.

Ashton moves his head off my neck to allow the collar to be taken off. The older human reaches into the back and picks me up lightly, ignoring my whines of protests. Ashton barks at him angrily, growling, and jumps out of the Ute heavily. He's so big he reaches up to the human's head, though he hunches down a little to look smaller.

I get carried inside into a very medical looking room, and get placed on a hard, silver table. It's cold, and makes me flinch away from it.

Ashton stands up on his hind legs and leans against the table. I shuffle forwards and press my nose into his chest, which is a high as I can reach.

Ashton watches over me almost possessively as I lie on the table, shivering and shaking and still teary eyed. I feel like a mess.

The humans both come back into the room. The older one stretches out my back legs, testing how sore I am.

I whimper when pain starts to hit my muscles. Ashton growls.

The older human feels through my tangled fur where I was cut. He winces a little. "Pass me the bandage will you, Blake." He says, holding his hand out.

Blake, the younger human, hands him a roll of bandages. "Here, Tim. What's wrong with her?"

"Nothing too bad. Just a cut." Tim answers.

I wait until Tim has finished bandaging the cut, tense and stiff. When he finishes, I slink off the table and drop onto the floor. I crawl over to the corner of the room and curl up there, trying to be as small as possible. I want my Mummy and Daddy, but they aren't ever going to come back and get me. They are dead. Gone.

Ashton drops back onto four paws and pads over to me. He squishes in behind me and puts his leg over my body comfortably. I try to hide in the curve of his body, feeling even smaller than before.

I close my eyes and try to relax.

(Ashton's POV)

I felt undeniable rage at Jack for hurting my Rosy like that. Couldn't he see she was frightened out of her wits? She was crying her eyes out, for God's sakes!

So when she ran I ran after her, but she washed away her scent and ran down wind. I couldn't find her, and I had started freaking out. When her pleading howls reached my ears I had felt a spark of hope and worry. Maybe I hadn't lost my little mate.

When I found her she was stuck under a thick log. There were two humans trying to help, and I wondered why they were out here. They were too weak to get the log off her, so I did. I could physically feel the fright pulsing off her.

There was a cut down Rosy's back and it was obvious her back half was bruised.

I only let the humans take her because it would raise suspicion if I took her back to my house. Plus it would do her some good if they bandaged her up. It would take me at least an hour to get back to my house with her, so I figured she should be looked at sooner rather than later.

Now she's curled up in a corner on the floor with a bandage around her thin middle area. I sit behind her, still in wolf form, and let my leg fall over her comfortably. She whimpers and pushes back into me, trying to hide in the curve of my body.

I start licking her head, an automatic instinct to help her calm down and start cleaning her fur.

I am still confused about why she was crying and why her heart was beating so fast. It's puzzling. To say I am worried for Rosy would be an understatement. I get that Jack was protecting his new mate, but he should always be careful around Rosy. She is maturing, sure, but she doesn't know better quite yet. She probably just wanted comfort.

A little rumble has my ears perking up. Is Rosy hungry?

"Did her stomach just growl?" The younger of the two humans, Blake, asks.

"I think it did." The older human, Tim, says with amusement in his voice.

Rosy whimpers and tucks herself closer into me. She turns her big baby blues up on me. I can pretty much feel my heart melt at the helpless look in her eyes.

A whining noise comes from me as I nudge her gently.

"Blake, can you go get some food from the back fridge? There should be something in there for them to eat. Anything red." Tim says.

Blake disappears into the back room as Tim cleans up the things he used to patch up Rosy.

A moment later Blake comes back into the room with food.

Rosy's ears perk up, though she stays close to me.

I probably wouldn't let her go even if she tried to move anyway.

(Rosy's POV)

I watch as Blake comes back into the room from the backroom. I'm very hungry. So hungry my stomach had started growling. By keeping my thoughts on my hunger, it prevents me from thinking of the nightmare I had. I don't want to think of my parents possibly being murdered. That dream just felt all too real for my likings.

Blake cuts up some of the red meat with a knife into smaller bite sized pieces for me and chucks one in front of me. It lands a few feet away from my face, but I really don't want to get up and hurt my back and legs. They are aching enough as it is. So I lazily put my head back down on my paws and look away.

Ashton stands up effortlessly and steps towards the small piece of meat. He leans down and sniffs it once, before picking it up and putting it in front of me.

I hungrily swallow it down, before looking up at Ashton who is sitting next to me on his haunches. He watches me with his warm, chocolate brown eyes. I rub my head against his leg thankfully, grateful for his help.

"Did he seriously just do that?" Blake asks, frowning with a strange emotion like disdain but amusement.

"I believe he did." Tim answers with the hint of a laugh in his voice.

"He is so whipped!" Blake laughs, watching Ashton with bright amused eyes. I wonder what that means.

Ashton snarls at him, shifting in front of me protectively. His fur brushes against mine softly. I can feel the heat pulsing off him. It's nice and comforting.

"Quieten down, Blake." Tim advises softly, his voice quieter.

I nudge Ashton with my nose gently, still kind of hungrily. I sniff the air once; still smelling meat on the table I was previously lying on.

Blake throws another piece at us.

The same thing as before happens again.

Ashton leans down and sniffs it. Picks it up and brings it to me. I eat it hungrily, scoffing it down like a pig. This happens many times over and over until my stomach is bulging from fullness. I feel a sleepy warmth start taking over me.

Ashton brings me another piece and sits down, but I nudge it with my nose back towards him. He must be hungry too, right? I can't be a hog and eat all the food by myself; he has to eat as well. He has to have some too. Mum always said it was good for me to share.

"Look at her! She's so full she looks like a big blonde snowball!" Blake laughs, looking at me.

Ashton growls at him, an angry tone to his voice.

"Don't insult his female!" Tim says, smacking Blake upside the head, but not too hard.

"His female?" Black asks wearily, kind of confused.

"Well she's obviously not related to him." Tim snorts disdainfully. "She hasn't got a spot of black on her, unlike him. They are too different to be related in any way. She must be in his pack or something. Why else would he be so protective of her?"

Blake nods once. "I suppose so. So do I feed him too?" He asks.

I growl, a strangely protective sound coming from me like when Ashton growls.

"I think you better." Tim says purposely.

Blake starts throwing much bigger bits at Ashton as he eats them. Ashton is still sitting up, so I crawl between his front paws and lie down there and slowly start relaxing. My fears get pushed to the back of my mind for now, along with the soreness in my heart I felt when Jack yelled at me.

I close my eyes and let an unwanted, restless sleep overtake me.

(Ashton's POV)

Rosy crawls between my front legs as I continue eating the meat they throw at me. What? I'm hungry and the meat is nice and sweet. I am half wolf after all. I listen to Rosy's heart beat as she falls into a twitchy and fitful sleep.

Something really must have scared her. This is one of the times I wish she was in my pack or I had marked her as my mate so I could speak with her through mind-link.

I look over at the door.

I want to get home so I can get Rosy to rest in a secure area. She needs to be safe. I want her to be able to relax and feel comforted. I want to know why she was so frightened. I want her to trust me enough to be able to confide in me.

"I don't think he wants to stay here." Blake says.

Where obviously, I snort to myself.

"Then we should let then go." Tim replies.

"What? Why?"

"Do you want to be stuck here with two angry wolves? Even one that is the size of a dog?" Tim asks.

I growl at his insult to my mate. My wolf doesn't like anyway saying bad or incriminating things about his Rosy.

"I guess not. But they're kinda cool, don't you think? It's not known that wolves are out in that forest." He says.

"And that's the way it should stay." Tim says. "If anyone found out there were wolves in the forest, they would be hunted down and captured, then probably separated."

I growl quietly. No one is separating me and Rosy. Not on my watch.

"So just let them go?" Blake asks.

"Yes." Tim opens the door.

My ears flick forwards. I lean down and pick Rosy up by the scruff of her neck. Because she is so small and I am so big, it's easy for me to carry her. She stirs and looks around with her sleepy blue eyes.

I walk outside the clinic surrounded by forest and put her down lightly. She whimpers in pain a little as her bruised body gets moved.

I nudge her forwards gently. She starts jogging slowly; testing out how sore her hips and hind legs are, with me following right after her. I turn my head back once to nod at the two humans slowly, who beam back at me happily.

I turn back around to run after my little mate.

Chapter Twelve

Sorry for the long wait, I was busy with exams and I didn't have much time to write. i think this one is a tad shorter than the other chapters... sorry :)

Hope you enjoy!!

Oh, and a BIG THANKS to all my new fans :) :)

Oh, one more thing. The spacing is screwing up in this a lot, which annoys me :(I'm trying to fix it, but it isn't really working.

*Recap ends at 'I turn back around to run after my little mate'. Again, the spacing is screwing up... sorry...

Recap:

(Ashton's POV)

My ears flick forwards. I lean down and pick Rosy up by the scruff of her neck. Because she is so small and I am so big, it's easy for me to carry her. She stirs and looks around with her sleepy blue eyes.

I walk outside the clinic surrounded by forest and put her down lightly. She whimpers in pain a little as her bruised body gets moved.

I nudge her forwards gently. She starts jogging slowly; testing out how sore her hips and hind legs are, with me following right after her. I turn my head back once to nod at the two humans slowly, who beam back at me happily.

I turn back around to run after my little mate.

Leading Rosy back home takes a long time.

She is in pain, and I don't like that. So I make her walk slowly, make her adjust to having bruised hips and legs. I don't want her to open the cut on her side, either.

So I make her be careful.

If there is a dip in the ground, or a rock in the way, or a log across her path, I do something about it. I lead her away from it, around it, or I carry her by the ruff of her neck.

I just don't want her move hurt than she already is. She's my mate; what can I say?

It's getting late and we are just barely half way there. I look down at Rosy and notice how tired she is. She's even dragging her paws under her.

Reaching over I pick her up by the scruff of her neck again and carry her through the trees. She yelps in surprise, but doesn't do anything to get out of my hold. I carry her to a small outcropping of rocks that are sticking out of the ground.

I put Rosy down in a small crevice that is hidden from the views of others at most angles. It's very secure and safe. I lie down in front of her and put my head down. She does as well.

Soon enough we both fall asleep.

When I wake up, the sun is shining on my back and there isn't any wind blowing through the trees. Rosy is still asleep, so I decide to leave her like that.

Standing up as quietly as possible, I lope away from the rocks in search of food for Rosy. It's not that hard to do, food around here is very plentiful.

Ten minutes later I am trotting back to Rosy with a rabbit hanging from my jaws. It doesn't feel safe leaving her alone, so I want to get back to her as fast as I can.

When the outcropping of rocks comes into view, my eyes immediately look for my Rosy. She is awake now. Rosy is cowering right back against the rocks, her body shaking a little. Her eyes dart around everywhere and her ears are upright and flicking back and forth.

I dart up to her, feeling worried and guilty.

Her eyes flicker over to me, before she whines quietly.

I hope she doesn't think I left her. I wouldn't ever leave her, not even for a second. If I had my way she wouldn't ever be more than a metre away from me.

I drop the rabbit in front Rosy and crowd around her, letting her tuck herself under my head against my chest. My tail curls around her as she sits in front of me, still shaking. Using my paw I pull the rabbit closer. The small animal would barely be a bite for me, but it is big enough to sate Rosy for a few hours.

She shakes her head, turning it back to look at me. She growls quietly, lashing out to nip my shoulder.

I yelp as a tiny stinging feeling comes to my shoulder.

But before I can do anything about it, Rosy nuzzles into my chest again. She licks my shoulder once, and almost instantly the pain disappears. She puts her head in the fur under my head, making a purring sort of sound.

Ok, I'm confused.

First she sits with me, then she bites me, then she cuddles with me?

Still very confused here.

I push the rabbit towards her again. She's got to eat to keep up her strength. Rosy lies down between my front legs to eat the rabbit after I sit up.

She finishes the food and nudges away the carcass. With a full yawn she rolls into me. I chuckle at her. She seems so lazy but it's so cute and adorable.

I stand up and stretch, Rosy doing the same.

We start heading back home.

(Rosy's POV)

It was really kind of Ashton to go and get food, but he could have taken me with him instead of leaving me alone. I thought he had left me by myself, and that made my heart hurt for some reason. I was scared of being alone.

But then when he came back with a rabbit in his mouth I had felt slightly better. I was still scared, but I felt a little better.

Then I felt a little annoyed, so I bit him on his shoulder.

But then I felt guilty for hurting him so I calmed down and nuzzled my face in the fur under his head.

And now he is leading me back to... somewhere. I'm not sure where, but I follow him anyway. I feel safer with him.

My back and hind legs still feel sore. I think they are bruised. At least the cut on my back has healed now, though the bandage is a little annoying. I stop to pull it off with my teeth, before walking a little faster to catch up to Ashton.

Later that day familiar smells start coming to my nose. We are on Ashton's pack's territory. Near his home. Where Jack lives.

I skid to a halt and put my butt down on the ground. I don't want to go back and see him. I am mad at him for yelling at me for no reason. I don't like being yelled at.

Ashton stops when he's realised I've sat down. He turns his big furry face back at me and cocks his head to the side a little.

I shake my head at him. No, I am not going back in there is Jack is going to yell at me again. I don't even know what I did wrong. I was just scared.

Ashton seems to sigh. He walks over to me and starts nudging me in a different direction.

I let him lead me away, wondering what he is doing. He leads me to tree, before making me lie down. He puts one of his paws on my back heavily, making me give him a confused look.

He backs away a little.

I whine, starting to follow after him. He comes forward again and pushes me back down to the ground. I get the message, so I make myself more comfortable. I put my head down on my paws and look up at him.

Ashton rubs his head against mine briefly, before turning and loping off in the direction of his house swiftly. I watch him go with a sinking feeling in the pit of my stomach. I curl up closer to the tree, feeling suddenly alone.

I guess that being with Ashton for the last day and a half made me miss his company when he's gone.

I look around. I don't recognise the place I am in. I never got his close to the house when I was out here for the past ten years. I was further out in Ashton's territory.

I look around. Everything seems darker. Like my dream. Every little noise is louder to my sensitive ears. The wind ruffles my fur. A new scent comes to my nose. A sour, dirty scent.

I stand up, my ears flicking back and forth and my eyes alert. I lean up against the tree, looking around for the wolf I smell. I growl, not liking the trapped feeling I feel.

The bushes in front of me rustle as the smell becomes stronger. Another growl rips through my chest, an angry growl.

A huge wolf -though not as big as Ashton- stalks out of the trees, his teeth bared.

I snarl, backing away from him. He doesn't seem safe. He looks scary.

The rogue wolf snarls back at me. He starts circling around me, as if he were stalking me like I would stalk a rabbit.

I take a step back away from him, suddenly wishing for Ashton's aura of safety to be around me. I want the comfort he gives me.

I let out a loud, daunting howl.

The rogue aims an infuriated howl at me.

He lunges.

Tell me if you spot any mistakes :)

Chapter Thirteen

Sorry about the long wait. I was very distracted over these last few weeks :) Anime is really addictive! Anyways, I tried to make this a little longer than the last one, so hopefully you guys like it.

Enjoy!

xox

Recap:

I snarl, backing away from him. He doesn't seem safe. He looks scary.

The rogue wolf snarls back at me. He starts circling around me, as if he were stalking me like I stalk a rabbit.

I take a step back away from him, suddenly wishing for Ashton's aura of safety to be around me. I want the comfort he gives me.

I let out a loud, daunting howl.

The rogue aims an infuriated howl at me.

He lunges.

I yelp and duck under his large, brown furred body, scampering away before he has a chance to turn and leap at me again. I howl once more, an urgent sound, calling for Ashton.

I hear a howl in reply; one I know comes from him.

The growl coming from the rogue werewolf abruptly stops. His ears perk up as he listens to Ashton howl, before he growls a me again. He springs at me again, and this time I can't dodge his teeth. His jaws clip my shoulder, making me cry out in pain.

I bark at him, which turns into a growl. My head whips out so that my tiny jaw can attempt to wrap around his neck, but I can barely reach halfway. Instead I end up with a mouthful of fur and a little bit of skin.

I skip back away from him before he can grab onto me and shake me like a ragdoll. I stand in front of a tree again, drawing myself to full height -which isn't much.

I growl defensively again, my fur bristling and standing on end. My shoulder starts to hurt, and my back half is still aching too. Especially my back legs. I growl at the rogue.

He growls back, stalking closer again, reading for another attack.

Another snarl enters the mix, making my heart leap and the rogue cower.

I run for the new voice.

Ashton steps out from the shadows, growling, angry beyond belief. He drops the clothes in his mouth -I notice some are my new ones. Ashton steps in front of me protectively, his brown eyes darkening so they almost blend into his black fur.

I hide behind him, feeling weak but safe.

More growls come from behind me, making me jump and squish into Ashton's side.

Two wolves, both a mixture of greys and whites, but none black like Ashton, are accompanied by a dark blonde wolf, darker than me.

When Ashton does nothing about them, I figure out that they are from his pack. I should have realised it before, the dark blonde wolf is Jack.

I turn my head away from him. I am still not happy with him. He was mean to me. He yelled at me when I was already crying.

The three new wolves lunge at the rogue as he turns and runs off with his tail between his legs.

Ashton turns his head back and nudges me gently, an apologetic noises coming from him. He licks the side of my head slowly, a remorseful gesture.

I lean down and pull my clothes apart from Ashton's, nudging his towards his paws. He picks them up, like I pick mine up and leads me behind thick trees and bushes. He leaves me on my own to shift back while he moves behind another tree.

I dump my clothes and slowly manage to turn back to a human. It's still uncomfortable to be on two legs; I like wolf form better. I pull my clothes on as quickly as I can.

I crouch down in the bushes, my eyes surveying the area for danger. When I don't see anything, I start to make my way towards where Ashton went. I realise that I don't feel safe without him around.

I creep closer until I see Ashton pulling a shirt on over his head. I dart up to him and crush my face into his chest. My arms go around his torso to clench the back of his shirt.

Ashton hugs me tightly. He rests his head in top of mine. "Are you alright, angel?" His voice is soft, quiet.

A little noise comes from the back of my throat. I clench my fists tighter. My shoulder starts stinging.

Ashton puts his arms under my knees and around my back before easily picking me up as if I were as light as a feather. He starts walking, able to carry me and not stumble at all.

A few minutes later he gets to his house. He carries me upstairs to his bedroom and places me gently on his bed.

He watches me for a second. "Are you hurt?" He asks.

I nod. "My shoulder." I whisper.

Ashton's eyes flash and his lips set in a thin line, but he doesn't say anything. He pushes down the collar of my shirt. I turn my head to look at my shoulder. There is a long blue and red bruise aligned with my shoulder bone, standing out against my pale skin. At least it isn't bleeding.

A little growl bursts out from Ashton. He brushes his fingers over the bruise, making me wince in pain.

"I've got to go and be with my pack." Ashton tells me, sighing and standing up.

Tears fill the corners of my eyes. "Don't leave me!" I cry, reaching for his hand.

His warm hand is bigger than mine, and pretty much swallows mine whole. It's rough, but soft at the same time.

Ashton squeezes my hand in his. "I'm not going to be long." He says softly, watching me with his bright brown eyes.

"I don't want to be alone." I whisper.

Ashton's gaze wavers. He sits back on the bed with me and pulls me into his arms. He rests his head on top of mine. "I won't be gone long, angel. I'm Alpha; I have to fulfil my duties to my pack. I promise I won't be gone long."

Tears fill my eyes, spilling over when I blink. "No! Please don't leave me!" I cry again, clenching my fists in his shirt. "Please." I add, quieter this time. My heart starts pounding faster at the thought of being all alone.

"Angel, I can't..." He murmurs, stroking my wild hair flat with his hand. His voice is pained and stiff as he tightens his arms around me.

I whimper quietly, squeezing my eyes shut.

A knock on the door makes me jump and Ashton growl. He tucks me in against his chest tighter and puts his arms around my waist.

I wonder who is at the door, but I don't really care. I don't want to be alone. I want to stay with Ashton. I want him to stay with me.

"Ashton, honey?" A very feminine voice asks from the door.

I stiffen. She sounds a lot like my Mum does- I mean did.

Ashton rubs my back instinctively. "Yeah Mum?" He sighs.

His Mum? I peek up over Ashton's shoulder quickly and see a woman with shoulder-length brown hair and blue eyes like Amy's standing in the doorway nervously.

"I couldn't help but overhear... do you want me to stay with Rosy?" She offers.

I feel Ashton look up in surprise. "Could you? Please?" He asks quietly, a pleading tone to his voice.

His Mother smiles softly. "Of course." She says.

Ashton takes my face in one of his hands, making me look up at him. "Is that alright with you?"

Watery tears spill down my face. "You're going to come back?" I ask anxiously.

He gives me a small, reassuring smile. "Yes, of course I'm going to come back." He says softly.

I sniff but nod, slowly detaching my hands from his shirt. He leans down as he stands and presses a kiss against my forehead, making sparks erupt from him skin to mine.

He leaves the room with a pained expression.

I start crying again. Ashton's Mum rushes forwards and envelopes me in a soft hug. Her scent is quite like Ashton's, but more feminine, with a softer undertone.

I end up crying myself to sleep.

(Ashton's POV)

Leaving Rosy with my Mum was the hardest thing I've ever done. My entire body hurt when I saw her watery eyes and terrified expression. I still need to know what happened to her and get a doctor to check her bruises.

But my pack is high on my priority list. They need to know what is happening with all these rogue attacks.

When I get downstairs, everyone that is present is waiting in the lounge room. My pack is large; there isn't really enough room, so only the adults and elderly came. And by elderly, I mean the eldest of our people.

Werewolves are exactly immortal, but once the mating process is complete our aging slows down quite dramatically.

Anyway, the people who hear what I say will carry the message among the rest of the pack members. Kind of like Chinese-whispers, but no one here is stupid enough to change the message.

"Alright, people!" I call over the chattering bunch, hushing everyone. "It seems as if the rogue attacks are becoming more and more frequent."

Almost immediately noise fills the room once more.

"Who are they targeting?" Someone calls over the noise.

Everyone quietens. "They are targeting a girl." I start of slowly, wondering how much to say at the moment. "Most of you should remember when Jackson stumbled onto our territory. His entire family had been slaughtered. His sister was missing." I say.

Every nods their heads.

"Well, the girl is his sister. She was stuck out in the forest for ten years, and is currently staying here. She was traumatized by something, and locked in the state of mind she was at that age. She thought she was six, but she's sixteen. Now while she may be maturing quickly, she is still frightened by new people who don't smell like Jack or my family. No one can go near here until she is ready." I say firmly.

Uproars of annoyance swell over the crowd. People want to know why they weren't told of Rosy and why they can't suss her out, which makes my wolf angry.

I fight back his protectiveness. Talking over the noise, I say, "You have to understand. She was lost for ten years, ten years. She was in her wolf form of all that time, resulting in a stunt in her growth. Her wolf is smaller than a normal wolf, and she's quite a small girl. She looks sixteen, but she still acts young. She gets frightened around other people." I argue.

The murmurs stop.

"I am sorry you did not know about her when we found her, but her frail state stopped me from telling you all. If you saw her when she came here all battered and bruised you would have acted the same way." I say.

"So is she the target of the rogues?" Someone asks.

I nod. "Yes. So far she has been attacked and injured three times on separate occasions and approached once. The rogues want her, and not for a good reason." I growl.

More growls join mine.

"We have to protect her from the rogues. She is Jack's sister, she is family. She has a kind heart and warm personality, and would not endanger anyone. She wouldn't hurt a fly. She is special." I say.

"So what can we do?" Someone asks.

"We have to train. The rogues are stopping at nothing to get a chance to hurt and possibly kill Rosy. We have to be aware of attacks and tighten security on our borders. I will warn the neighbouring packs, but everyone has to be wary. I want no one out hunting or running alone. Four to a group, more if possible. No one is to go out alone with less than four people without telling me first. I want mind-link to always be open to me if you exit the neighbourhood and when you are in wolf form." I demand.

Everyone nods.

"Any questions?" I ask. A few hands go up. I point to a woman near the back.

"Are we going to ever meet Jack's sister?" She asks.

I become a little defensive. "When she feels like she can act comfortably around pack members, I'll bring her to one of the pack bonfires." I say.

Another person asks a question. "Why is she only comfortable around people who smell like Jack or you?" He asks.

"Well, for one, Jack is her family and the only person she remotely recognised. She trusts him fully, so she is comfortable around him." I say.

"Well what about you?"

"I was the first person she met, and along with other fighters I protected her from the attacks." I say.

"So she trusts you?"

"Yes." I nod.

"Is she going to join this pack?" A woman asks.

"If she wants to when she's ready, she can. That's if the majority of the pack accepts her, of course." I add through half grated teeth. "Any more questions?" I ask. One more hand goes up.

"Do you know how many rogues there are all together? Do you know what they are doing or why they are going after Rosy?" A man asks.

"We don't know how many rogues there are. We are assuming there is a lot, though. They mostly attacked in bands of four, or alone. We don't know why they are going after Rosy in particular, but it could have something to do with her parents' death." I say.

I wait to see if there are any more questions, but everyone stays quiet.

"Right, meeting dismissed." I say hurriedly, wanting to get back to Rosy.

I wait until every member of my pack that was here to leave, before finally relaxing a little. I turn around and race back up the stairs and down the hallway to my room.

I rip open the door and look straight to my bed. I see Rosy curled up with my Mum, her head on my Mum's shoulder and her small hands clutching her shirt. Her eyes are scrunched closed with pain as tears still stream down her face. My Mum is watching her, rocking her softly like she would rock one of the pack children. I can see my Mum has already formed a bond with Rosy.

I feel my chest constrict. Walking forwards slowly, I sit on the edge of my bed without taking my eyes off Rosy's sleeping form.

"She cried herself to sleep." Mum tells me quietly, after a moment of silence, making me grimace.

"Can I have her?" I ask, reaching my arms out for Rosy.

Mum hands her over, gently prying Rosy's fingers from her shirt.

Rosy whimpers at the brief lack of human contact, before gripping onto my shoulder and resting in my lap. As soon as her skin touches mine, the same familiar sparks erupts and makes me smile to myself. It's quite a relaxing feeling, those sparks.

Mum watches my every movement as I shift Rosy into a more comfortable position with her legs by my sides and her head on my shoulder.

I smile a little as Rosy stops crying quietly and starts sleeping peacefully.

Mum watches me carefully. "Is she your mate, Ashton?" She asks suddenly.

I stiffen a little. "Why would you think that?" I ask. What? It's kind of embarrassing talking to your own mother about that sort of thing. I don't want her asking about when her grandchildren are going to come, geez!

"Well, for one you have never, and I mean never, even touched a girl like you hold Rosy. Another thing is that you keep protecting her, and you ran after her two days ago. You smile when she is around, and you haven't smiled like that since Diana and your Father passed away." She says.

I sigh. "Yeah, she is my mate." I confess, smiling to myself when I admit it out loud. It sounds… just perfect.

A full blown smile lights up my Mum's face. "I knew it." She grins. "She seems like such a sweet child. Is she going to mature, though?" Mum asks.

"She has already, a little. She's not as… childish, I guess, as before. All she needs is time." I reply, running my fingers through her long, tangled hair. Rosy murmurs something in her sleep.

Mum nods. "You really seem to like her, Ashton. Don't scare her away; we all know you can be intimidating at times." She warns.

I growl as a protective feeling creeps into my chest. "I wouldn't ever scare her." I say as my arms tighten around her subconsciously. She makes a small noise in the back of her throat, rubbing her face against my shoulder and into the crook of my neck as she finds a more comfortable position. Almost straight away my body and expression softens as I watch her curiously.

Mum gives me a small smile. A proud smile. "That's good to know, Ashton. Protect your mate, because without her your life is hardly worth living. Trust me, I know." Mum gives me a rueful smile, obviously thinking about Dad.

Just before she leaves the room, I ask her a question. "Why do you live on? What's your reason, Mum?" I ask quietly.

"Well I have you kids. I have to make sure you keep the pack in line." She replies softly, watching me with her blue eyes. The same eyes Amy has.

I chuckle. "We do love you, Mum." I tell her.

"I know. I love you guys too." She smiles, before leaving the room and shutting the door behind her.

I turn my attention back to Rosy.

She seems so peaceful when she sleeps, less worried about everything she does.

I rest my head on hers and wait for her to wake up.

Chapter Fourteen

I really like this chapter, hope you do to :) I've already started on the next chapter, so hopefully the wait will be a little less than 2 weeks.

Enjoy!

xox

Recap:

I chuckle. "We do love you, Mum." I tell her.

"I know. I love you guys too." She smiles, before leaving the room and shutting the door behind her.

I turn my attention back to Rosy.

She seems so peaceful when she sleeps, less worried about everything she does.

I rest my head on hers and wait for her to wake up.

(Rosy's POV)

My body feels warmer when I wake up. I'm not as cold as I was when I went to sleep. I sit up straighter, finding myself still tangled in someone's arms. I expect to see Ashton's Mum holding me like when I went to sleep. But when I look up I see Ashton holding me, fast asleep. He's still sitting up, and so am I. I grin. He came back!

"Ashton!" I cry, throwing my arms around his neck.

He jumps awake as the force of my hug knocks him back onto the bed with me on top. He laughs as I squeeze the life out of him. "Good afternoon, angel." He murmurs, nuzzling his face into the crook of my neck.

I giggle as his hair tickles my throat. "Stop it, that tickles!"

He chuckles, sitting back up and tightening his arms around me.

"Wait, did you say afternoon?" I ask, frowning in confusion.

He nods.

"I slept all day?"

"Yes, and apparently so did I." He chuckles again.

"What day is it?" I ask.

"It's Tuesday." He says.

I nod, resting my head on his shoulder again.

"Isn't today the day your Mum always used to brush your hair?" He asks me.

"You remembered?" I ask, shocked.

A small smile splays across his lips. "Of course I did." He tells me as if it were the most obvious thing in the world.

I smile and turn my face into his throat. "Can you do it now instead?" I ask nervously, wondering if he will do it or not.

Ashton grins. "I would love to." He replies, brushing his fingers down my back over my shirt. I shiver a little, subconsciously.

Ashton puts his arm under thighs as he stands up. He sets me down on the edge of the bed before walking to his bedside table. He opens the top draw and pulls out Diana's pretty brush again. He moves to sit behind me like last time, with one of his legs on either side of me.

I lean forwards a little, letting him have better access to my long hair. It's quite tangled.

Just like last time, he sets the brush down beside my leg and starts untangling the knots in my hair with his fingers. It's very calming.

"Can you tell me about Diana?" I ask quietly, not wanting to upset him.

Ashton stiffens behind me, but his body softens when I rest my hand on his knee.

I wait to see if he will speak or not.

"Diana was my older sister. She was the spitting image of my Mum, with brown hair and blue eyes, but she was a complete Daddy's girl. She did everything with my Dad, like Amy, whereas I was a Mummy's boy." Ashton starts.

I nod, feeling his fingers run through parts of my long blonde hair.

"Diana loved shopping. It was her favourite thing to do. She loved buying clothes for everyone, including me, though I hated it. She loved brushing her hair and doing her nails. She loved doing anything girly. She enjoyed running in the forest with Amy and I, too." Ashton says.

I can hear the smile in his voice.

"Diana always had high grades and always kept up with her image. Diana had heaps of friends, it was impossible to not like her. Everyone enjoyed her company. Though she didn't have a mate, she wanted one. She wanted to get married and have three kids, was it? Yeah. She wanted to have a peaceful life with three little kids running around." Ashton continues.

Diana sounds like someone I would like.

"She was very protective of the pack. She was defending three of the younger teenagers who were fighting four of the rogues when she died. She managed to kill them all before her body gave out." Ashton says, his voice quiet and sad.

I twist around in his arms and wrap my arms around his neck. I press my lips to his cheek as an act of condolence. It may have been the lighting, but I swear I see his cheeks redden.

"I like Diana." I say, turning back around to sit straight again. When I say her name, it sounds very childish. I'm starting to want to be older.

Ashton picks up the brush and starts pulling it through my hair lightly. He doesn't say anything, but the silence is comfortable. I close my eyes and just enjoy the feeling of my hair being played with.

"Are we starting school tomorrow?" I ask quietly.

"Yes, once the doctor checks you over." He replies just as quietly.

I nod.

A while later he sets the brush down on the bed and puts his arm under my knees and around my back. He picks me up and takes me out of his room. I expect him to take me back to mine and Amy's room, but he takes me down the stairs and to the lounge room.

I give him a confused look as he sits on the sofa with his legs crossed and me in his lap.

"The guys are going to move your bed into my room... if that's ok with you?" Ashton asks, kind of nervously.

I let out a sigh of relief. "That's good." I say firmly.

Ashton gives me a small, relieved smile and rests his head on mine.

"You don't mind me sleeping in your room?" I ask him quietly.

"No, not at all." Ashton says quickly, sounding happier.

I smile and turn my face into his chest.

(Ashton's POV)

"You don't mind me sleeping in your room?" Rosy asks me, her voice quiet.

"No, not at all." I answer quickly, happy.

I feel Rosy smile as she turns her face into my chest. I don't think she knows it, but her hand was gripping my shirt and her cheeks were constantly a rosy pink colour.

I was listening to some of the pack members' upstairs move Rosy's bed into my room when the front door opens and shuts.

Rosy stiffens as Jack's scent wafts down the hallway. A frightened whimper comes from her, making me growl possessively. I tighten my arms around her as she curls up in my lap. I don't think she's ready to face her brother just yet, not after he scared her so much. I still need to ask her why she ran, but I'll leave that conversation for a later time.

"What happened?" I ask, quite formally, when Jack and the fighters come into the room.

"That rogue's not going to be running around anymore." One of the fighters says.

I nod, getting his message. "Did you spot anything else?" I ask.

"No." The other says, shaking his head.

"Ok, you can go." I say, dismissing them.

Jack stays, though. "Rosy?" He says tentatively, staring hard at my perfect little mate.

She gulps and turns further into my chest, whimpering quietly. I can feel nerves radiating off her.

Another protective feeling slams into me as she makes that frightened noise once again. I curl her small body into my chest while glaring at Jack. My wolf doesn't like his mate being scared or apprehensive; he doesn't like it at all.

"Jack." I warn, my voice coming out as a low growl.

His eyes flick to mine as the air becomes tense.

Another constant animalistic growl rumbles from my chest, a sound that is filled with power and proves that I am Alpha.

He sighs, before leaving the room quietly.

Rosy relaxes in my arms and leans against me heavily. "Thank you." She says quietly, clutching my shirt tighter in her tiny fist.

"No problem." I answer just as quietly.

Upstairs I hear the guys all finish, before they come down the stairs quietly and leaving the house, probably thinking Rosy is asleep. It's nice to think that they are considerate of her, even though she isn't technically a part of the pack. Rosy doesn't even notice them leave.

Standing up, I tighten my grip on her. She is silent as I carry her back up the stairs. She weighs less than I would like her to. I set her down outside Amy's bedroom door.

"Change into your pyjamas then come to my room, yeah?" I say, absent-mindedly brushing hair out of her eyes.

She nods her head and walks into her room.

I turn down the hallway and walk to my room, half shutting the door behind me. I walk into my bathroom and change into my pyjama pants. I don't sleep with a shirt on, it's too uncomfortable. It makes me feel kind of boxed in.

I flop down on my bed, looking at Rosy's bed next to mine. A small smile comes to my lips. It's nice to know my mate is sleeping in my room where I can watch over her. Our room. It makes a warm feeling spread through my body.

The door creaks as it opens a little more as Rosy peeks her pretty little head in. I beckon her into the room with a flick of my wrist and she bounces in, closing the door behind herself.

She jumps on her bed and rolls on her stomach. She's wearing just a pair of purple pyjama pants and a white singlet that clings to her curvy body. She rests her chin on her hands and watches me.

I lie on my side facing her. "Want to tell me what scared you two days ago?" I ask softly.

She sighs, looking down. "I... I had a nightmare." She starts hesitantly.

"What about?"

"Well, I was in the forest and I was six. Actually six. Mum and Dad told me to stay quiet and to hide, so I did. But I got bored and ended up following after them after they had shifted to wolf form. They were in a small clearing when I found them." She continues.

I stay silent, just listening to her melodic voice, even if it is frightened.

"There were three men facing them, and they had guns. I cried out and my Mum shifted back to human form. She told me to run back and hide, but I didn't want to. I only left when she promised to come back and get me and the men started sneering at me. When I was leaving, I heard loud bangs so I raced back." She whispers.

I stay quiet again.

She takes in a deep breath, tears coming to the corner of her eyes. "I ran back and there was b-blood everywhere. There were two lumps on t-the ground and they w-weren't moving and when I r-ran over t-there they weren't breathing. Blood was all over their fur and they w-weren't b-breathing!" She practically screams hysterically, bursting into tears again.

I feel my heart squeeze at that. I open my arms and she immediately launches herself at me and starts crying in my chest. Her hands clutch at me as if she was drowning and I was her lifesaver. She seems so frail and broken and small when she cries like this, so devastated. It almost makes me want to cry.

"Shh, it's ok angel... shh..." I murmur, rubbing her back gently.

She just cries harder. "I s-sa-saw t-them a-and they w-weren't mov-moving!" She cries, her words hiccupping as she tries to breath properly.

No wonder she went to Jack for comfort. He's her only family, and then he goes and yells at her when she didn't do anything wrong! She must have been so scared. My annoyance at Jack just gets deeper and deeper. I can see why he protected his mate, because I am doing it now, but still. This is his baby sister we're talking about; she doesn't know what she did wrong.

I let Rosy cry it out. She needs a way a release for all of her built up emotions, and this is the way to do it. Crying always helps.

After a while she finally sniffs the last of her tears. "Can I sleep in your bed tonight?" She pleads, looking up at me with her big blue watery eyes. "Please?" She adds quietly, her bottom lip trembling.

I feel my expression soften. How can I say no to that expression? "Of course you can sleep here." I say softly, brushing my nose against hers in an attempt to make her happier.

She giggles, though her eyes are still watery, and I smile. Rosy nuzzles down into my chest, pulling her knees to her chest, one of her arms creeping around my waist. Her bare skin against mine makes me want to shiver with pleasure.

I hug her tighter as I wait for her to fall asleep. Listening to her steady breathing is calming, lulling me into that space between sleep and consciousness.

Soon enough Rosy's breathing evens out as she falls asleep with her lips slightly parted. She looks so peaceful when she is asleep.

I reach down for the covers and pull them up over our bodies, to make sure she doesn't get cold during the night. Only when I'm sure that she is content do I allow myself to fall asleep too.

With Rosalina.

Chapter Fifteen

Sorry for the long wait, my laptop broke so my access to wattpad and Word are now limited :(I will write as much as I can, and I will try to upload again within the next two weeks :)

Enjoy!! xox

Recap:

(Ashton's POV)

I feel my expression soften. How can I say no to that expression? "Of course you can sleep here." I say softly, brushing my nose against hers in an attempt to make her happier.

She giggles, though her eyes are still watery, and I smile. Rosy nuzzles down into my chest, pulling her knees to her chest, one of her arms creeping around my waist. Her bare skin against mine makes me want to shiver with pleasure.

I hug her tighter as I wait for her to fall asleep. Listening to her steady breathing is calming, lulling me into that space between sleep and consciousness.

Soon enough Rosy's breathing evens out as she falls asleep with her lips slightly parted. She looks so peaceful when she is asleep.

I reach down for the covers and pull them up over our bodies, to make sure she doesn't get cold during the night. Only when I'm sure that she is content do I allow myself to fall asleep too.

With Rosalina.

(Rosy's POV)

When I wake up I am still in Ashton's arms, facing his bare chest. The heat from his skin washes over me. I wonder why he doesn't sleep with a shirt on.

A sudden thought hits me. I get to finally start school today!

With an excited yelp I jump at Ashton and push him onto his back, startling him awake. He growls as his eyes snap open. He grabs me closer while at the same time pushing me way, which ends up making us roll over again until we fall off the bed.

I gasp in shock as my back leaves the bed. Ashton tightens his grip on me as he flips us over so he is below me when we hit the floor with a loud thump.

I grin foolishly at his extremely shocked face. "That was fun. Can we do it again?" I chirp happily.

He opens his mouth to say something, but nothing comes out. He tries to speak again, but again nothing comes out. Only his hands tighten on my hips. He ends up staring at me with his mouth hanging open.

I giggle. Reaching up, I put my hand on his chin and shut his mouth. "Stop doing that, you look like a goldfish." I say as sternly as I can, which only makes me sound like a child more than usual.

He grins up at me, making his brown eyes sparkle more.

"Now come on," I whine, "I want to start school!"

He chuckles at my eagerness, almost all traces of sleep gone from his face and body.

I get up off him while taking his hands and yanking him up with all my strength, which isn't very much. He ends up having to stand by himself since I'm not much help.

"Come on!" I get behind him and try to push him to move faster. It doesn't really work.

Ashton looks at the clock. "It's only seven in the morning! Not even the birds are up yet!" He complains.

"But I'm already up!" I counter, switching to grab his hand and drag him towards the door.

He doesn't budge again. He flops back down on the bed, tugging me down with him. I land on his chest making hum grunt. "Rosy! It's too early!" He grumbles, rubbing his eye with a fist that I am not holding.

I pout. "Please?" I stick out my bottom lip.

He peeks at me with one eye, before groaning again. "Rosy, you know I can't resist that face!" He protests.

I keep the face up, tugging on his hand gently, drawing his attention back to me.

He grunts, unable to keep his eyes off my face. "Fine."

I grin and drag him up again. I tow him out of the room by the hand while he stumbles along tiredly behind me. It would have looked strange to anyone who saw us to see a tiny girl dragging around a tall, muscled guy.

I am starting to know my way around Ashton's house. I know how to get from the front door to the kitchen, lounge room, up the stairs and too Amy's, Ashton's or Jack's room. I don't need to find the bathroom because I can use the one in Ashton's room.

When I get to the kitchen, Ashton's Mum is already up and making coffee and breakfast for herself.

"Good morning!" I sing, sitting on a stool at the bench and making Ashton sit next to me. He doesn't let go of my hand.

Ashton's Mum turns around. "Wow, you actually got him out of bed before lunch time." She says, shocked.

Ashton grunts again and bangs his forehead against the kitchen bench. It doesn't hurt him; he's a werewolf. He mumbles something about the birds not being up yet again.

Ashton's Mum laughed. "Aw, don't worry honey. You'll have to get used to it." She says, patting his head.

He groans. "How can anyone get up this early? Just kill me now." He mumbles, yawning.

His Mum chuckles.

I laugh at him.

He growls playfully and tightens his grip on my hand.

A warm shower, breakfast, and a large cup of coffee later and Ashton is finally ready to start tutoring me. I have had a shower and eaten, too. But I didn't really like Ashton's coffee, it needed more sugar. That didn't stop me from drinking the last bits, though.

Everyone who slept in this house last night had gotten up and got ready for school or work. Ashton and I are the only ones in the house now. I think Linda, Ashton's Mum, went out grocery shopping.

Ashton had taken me to a new room. It was set up like a classroom, but only smaller than a normal classroom, like the size of a normal bedroom. There is a long table in the centre of the room with chairs on either side of it, and a blackboard on the wall. There are wide windows that let in a lot of light and fresh air, too.

Ashton sits across the desk in front of me. He gave me a workbook and pencil case filled with school stuff. I like the highlighters.

Ashton was teaching me the alphabet and showing me how to write. He wrote the alphabet and put it in front of me. I can't help but notice how neat his writing is.

I pick up the pencil, wrapping my tiny fist around it. I try to write an 'a', but it doesn't work. I huff in frustration, my brow furrowing.

Ashton chuckles. "No, you hold it like this." He says, leaning over the table to move my fingers into a different position around the pencil. "Try it now." He says, watching me intently.

I admit, this is easier to write, but I can't seem to get the hang of writing the actual letter. I try until the first few lines in my book are filled, but nothing looks like the letter Ashton wrote.

I almost start crying in frustration. "I can't do it!" I say unhappily.

Ashton watches me carefully again. "Yes you can, come on Rosy." He urges gently.

I try for another line on the same letter, but it looks horrible. The pencil just keeps slipping and sliding all over the place like a soap bar in wet hands.

When I press harder and concentrate properly, my hand trembles and the letter ends up looking like a rock.

Again I almost start crying. I whimper in frustration, my grip on the pencil tightening.

Ashton, sensing my annoyance and disappointment, stands up and walks around to my side of the desk. He easily lifts me up, making me yelp, and sits in my chair with me on his lap. I immediately settle comfortably, an instant reaction.

Ashton reaches around me, wrapping his left arm around my waist while his right reaches for my writing hand. He puts his hand over mine.

"Like this." He says, moving my hand with his over it to make a perfect little 'a'.

My eyes widen. How'd he do that?

Ashton keeps his hand around mine as he guides my hand -and therefore the pencil- to do a whole line of 'a's.

"See? It's not the hard." He says, smiling.

I grin. Slowly, Ashton takes his hand away from mine. I continue writing the alphabet. While my writing isn't as neat as his, it is still kind of readable.

"Done." I say when I finish writing the last letter of the alphabet, the 'z'.

Ashton leans forwards and looks over at my work. He smiles and rests his chin on my shoulder. "Great job, Rosy. That's really good." He smiles at me.

I grin wider. "Maybe this isn't so hard."

Hours later when the sun was streaming right into the room and onto Ashton and me, I was finally starting to get tired. I was leaning up against

Ashton's chest, trying to focus on what he was teaching me. My head is starting to hurt from all this learning.

"Mhmm..." I mumble, nodding as if I were actually listening to him.

I rest my head back on his shoulder in the crook of his neck, my face turned towards his throat. I close my eyes and decide to take a rest from all this work. Hopefully Ashton won't notice.

(Ashton's POV)

I was teaching Rosy about the vowels when she leans back into my chest and puts her head in the crook of my neck. I almost shiver at the strange touch.

"Mhmm..." She mumbles, nodding. I can tell she's not listening to me, it's so obvious. She closes her eyes and soon enough her heartbeat steadies out into an even rhythm.

I smirk at her, though she can't see it. She's so predictably adorable and sweet. Not to mention gorgeous. Waking up to find her sitting on me and practically begging me with her bright blue eyes to start teaching her was the best wake-up call I've ever had. Most people know I hate mornings, and yet she got me up. My Mother thought that was hilarious.

I sigh, gently drawing circles on Rosy's stomach. She makes an unconscious purring noise of content. Well, her wolf does, appreciating the attention I give her even if she is asleep.

I sigh and settle myself around her, before falling asleep myself, content to have her in my arms. This afternoon nap can make up for the sleep I lost when I was forced to wake up at the crack of dawn.

I smile to myself as I fall asleep.

(Rosy's POV)

Ashton and I developed a routine over the next four days. In the morning I would forcefully wake him up and drag him downstairs, entertaining his mother every time. He would have his coffee, which I learned to like. I would always steal sips of it when he wasn't looking.

We would both shower, usually him first while I talk to Linda, and get dressed and have breakfast that Linda made for us. We would talk with her for a little while longer until everyone left for school and work before Ashton would start my schooling again.

I am proud to say I am a fast learner, or so Ashton says. I have been maturing quicker now, I can see it in myself. I don't feel six anymore, I feel... older.

The pack doctor, not Jack, checked me over on Wednesday night before dinner. She said I was just a little bruised, but I was healing just fine. My hips and legs don't hurt anymore, and neither does my back. I'm all good.

I haven't talked to Jack yet. Whenever he comes into the room or near me, I freak out and leave quickly, or Ashton tells him to leave. I have become very... clingy, I guess you could say, to Ashton. I don't really do anything without telling him first. He always comes with me when I run in wolf form in the afternoons, and I sleep in his room. Not that I mind. It's fun having him around.

While he can be serious and intimidating when he goes into protective alpha mode, he's never like that with me. He's always considerate of my feelings, and never ever yells at me. He's always nice and friendly.

It was the afternoon now, and Ashton and I had finished schooling for the day. I was sitting next to him on the sofa. He was holding one of my hands, idly playing with my fingers. My eyes are glued to the T.V.

"Hey Rosy." Ashton says, pulling on one of my fingers gently.

"Yeah?"

"Do you want to go for a run? Maybe with Amy?"

My eyes light up. "Yeah! Can we?"

Ashton smiles that dazzling smile again, making my stomach twist in little knots. "Of course."

"Then let's go!" I cry, twisting my hand in his to grip his and pull him up.

Ashton calls down Amy and leads us outside. We all spilt off into different directions and shift behind a tree, taking our clothes off first. Shifting is easier now for me, it doesn't make me uncomfortable to be in either form.

When I am in my light blonde wolf form, I race over to where Ashton was. He's just shifted, and is shaking out his midnight black fur. I jump at him, growling playfully, and tackle him. I know he falls by himself- I'm too small to do any actual damage to him. If he hadn't had fallen, I probably would have just rebounded off him.

I start chewing on one of his ears, still growling. It doesn't hurt him though.

Amy comes bounding towards us. She's got grey fur and dark blue eyes, so dark they look black, like in her human form. She is smaller than Ashton, seeing as he is Alpha and a male, but she is a lot bigger than me.

She jumps on Ashton too. He rolls out from under me and tackles Amy, pinning her to the floor with his big body. She submits quickly, making me snicker. I would too if I had Ashton's furry hide crushing me.

Ashton stands up properly and stretches, arching his back and letting Amy up. I move to stand beside Ashton, bumping up against him.

Ashton leads us as we run, since he knows the way the best. The trees soon enough blur past us in flashes of green and the wind whips back at my fur.

I love running.

Later that night, after dinner, Ashton, Amy and I were talking in Ashton's room. I am laying stomach first on my bed, while Ashton and Amy are sitting cross legged on Ashton's bed. Everyone has gotten changed into their pyjamas.

"So, do you like it here?" Amy asks, throwing me a chocolate MNM from the packet in her hand.

I nod, catching and eating the lolly.

"Do you think you will eventually join our pack?" She casually asks next.

I think about it for a moment, tilting my head to the side. "I think I will, eventually." I say, nodding. It would be good to belong to such a nice pack. It kind of gets lonely in my head when we go running since I can't use mind-link because I don't have anyone to chat with.

Out of the corner of my eye I see an unquestionably happy grin spread across Ashton's face. I wonder why he's so happy; maybe because I will join his pack.

A tired yawn comes from me, my hand fluttering up to cover my mouth.

"Ok, bedtime now." Ashton says.

"But I'm not tired!" I protest, trying to cover up another yawn.

He chuckles, and so does Amy.

"Good night, Rosy." Amy waves at me, smiling, before leaving the room and shutting the door behind her.

Ashton comes over and pulls the covers over my body. I know it will do no good for me to protest, which I did try one night. Ashton just smiles.

"Sweet dreams, Rosy." Ashton says, tucking me in. He leans down and presses his lips to my forehead, making those same sparks fill my entire body. I smile to myself.

"Night Ashton." I yawn again.

He moves to flick the light off before climbing into bed himself.

And like always, I fall asleep pretty quickly.

I wake up sweating with a fast beating heart. I had another nightmare.

A small whimpering sound comes from my throat. I kick the covers off me and swing my legs out of the bed. I slink over to Ashton's bed and crawl under the covers quietly.

He's fast asleep, facing me.

I scoot closer to him until I am curled up in his chest. I reach up to touch his cheek with my fingertips. He still doesn't wake up. I press my palm against his cheek.

Ashton mumbles something that I can't understand. His arms inch around my waist and pull me to his body. He buries his head in my hair, taking a deep breath and breathing out. His hands press against my back as he settles around me.

Just being near him helps me to calm down. I rest my head against his chest and fall asleep again.

Chapter Sixteen

Finally uploaded! Yay! I hop eyou like it!

Enjoy!! xox

Recap:

I wake up sweating with a fast beating heart. I had another nightmare.

A small whimpering sound comes from my throat. I kick the covers off me and swing my legs out of the bed. I slink over to Ashton's bed and crawl under the covers quietly.

He's fast asleep, facing me.

I scoot closer to him until I am curled up in his chest. I reach up to touch his cheek with my fingertips. He still doesn't wake up. I press my palm against his cheek.

Ashton mumbles something that I can't understand. His arms inch around my waist and pull me to his body. He buries his head in my hair, taking a deep breath and breathing out. His hands press against my back as he settles around me.

Just being near him helps me to calm down. I rest my head against his chest and fall asleep again.

(Ashton's POV)

Surprisingly, the next morning it wasn't Rosy who woke me up, it was my Mum. Usually it is Rosy wanting school to start early, but today it wasn't.

Mum doesn't bother knocking on the door. She knows that if it isn't locked she can come in if she wants to. That's the way it's been since Dad and Diana passed away.

I was still asleep when she came in, though I am close to waking up.

"Ashton. Rosy." She says, shaking me by the shoulder and probably Rosy as well.

When I hear a small grunt of sleepy annoyance, I subconsciously tighten my arms around... something. Someone.

That makes me jolt wide awake. My eyes fly open and when I look down I see Rosy curled in my arms, pressed against my chest. Her head is resting on my collarbone comfortably. Her arm is tightly slung over my torso; as if she were afraid I'd disappear and wanted to keep a hold on me. That thought makes me smile a little. I can feel that Rosy's hand is fisted at the small of my back.

"Aw, isn't that adorable?" My Mum coos.

I groan. "Mum." I whine, dragging the word out.

"What? It's nice to finally see my baby holding a pretty girl." She says.

"I'm not a baby anymore." I argue.

"You're a baby compared to me."

I huff. "Why are you waking me up?" I ask curiously.

"Well, you started schooling Rosy on Wednesday. That was five days ago, which means she's done a full school week, even if it went through the weekend. I was just thinking you guys needed a break, especially Rosy." Mum says, patting Rosy's hair down.

"You really like her, don't you?" I ask, watching my Mum stare at Rosy.

"I do." Mum sighs happily. "It's like having another child in the house. It's great that I get to watch her grow up and mature. It makes me make feel like I have known her for her entire life."

I smile to myself. It's a good feeling you get when your Mum likes your mate so much.

Rosy rolls over in her sleep, pressing her back against my chest. She turns her face into my pillow and takes a deep breath of my scent, making me smile at her.

"It's a Monday today. What are the two of you going to do?" Mum asks quietly, sitting on the edge of my bed. She doesn't seem bothered by the fact that I don't have a shirt on, but then again she never is.

"Whatever she wants, I guess." I shrug.

"That's cute!" My Mum says, making me feel embarrassed.

"Mum," I groan, "Please. I don't do anything 'cute'." I scoff.

"Ok." She sings. "If you say so." She says, standing up and leaving the room with a smirk on her face.

I roll my eyes at her as she closes the door again. My attention returns to Rosy. She's been maturing quite fast these last five days. I can't honestly wait until she's her proper age when she starts learning about werewolves. Especially the mates' part.

But waiting for her to grow up and waiting before even starting the mating process is actually kind of exciting. It feels good being able to wait for her, being able to build a solid foundation for our future relationship. I know I sound like a complete girl right now, but it's the truth.

I move one of my hands to touch her face lightly, marvelling at how smooth and soft her skin is. I never knew skin got so soft.

Rosy rolls over to face me again, still sleeping. It's easier to see and touch her face when she faces me. A yawn comes from her soft-looking pink lips as she slowly wakes up. A moment later and her mind seems to have cleared because she seems more alert.

"Good morning, angel." I smile down at her, loving having her curled up in my arms. It feels so... perfect.

She smiles back lazily. Then she looks at the position she's in. A pretty red blush spreads across her cheeks, making her look cuter than ever. I love making her blush. "Oh, um... uh?" She mumbles, looking down.

I chuckle, making her blush deepen. I bend my head a little and kiss each of her cheeks. "I don't mind having you here." I smile.

A relieved look comes to her face. She tucks her head under my chin, making my heart jump into my throat. Every little thing she does -like tuck her head under my chin, or kiss my cheek, or even hold my hand- seems so much more important than anything else. It's like the littlest things are the things I like the best.

"Is there anything you want to do today?" I ask her, brushing hair out of her eyes.

Her brow furrows as a confused expression comes to her face. "Like what? Isn't today a school day? Don't we have to work?" She asks, confused.

"Well, we worked through the weekend, which means we finished your first official school week. So my Mum and I thought it would be good to take the day off, you know? Have a break and have some fun." I explain.

"Oh, well that does make sense." She says thoughtfully, her mind wondering. I can't wait until she eventually joins my pack and I can speak with her through mind-link. It's going to be fun to be in her pretty little head. Then when I eventually mark her and we have the mate bond... all these thoughts are just so exciting. Like Christmas for a little kid.

"So is there anything you want to do in particular?" I ask again.

She thinks about it for a moment, before shaking her head. "I don't know." She says, looking up at me with her big baby blues.

"How about we go to the beach?" I suggest.

Her eyes light up. "Can we go?"

I smile down at her beautiful face. "Of course we can." I say, smiling again. I am finding it impossible not to smile around her. She's too adorably happy to be sad or worried around.

"Yay!" She exclaims, jolting out of bed and dragging me with her.

Did I forget to mention she is getting stronger and faster? "Ok, go get ready and I'll meet you downstairs for breakfast, yeah?" I say, urging her out of the room. All of her clothes and shoes are still in Amy's room.

Rosy darts out of the room and down the hallway. I watch her with curious eyes as she bolts into Amy's room, shutting the door behind her. Lucky we slept in and Amy's already gone to school otherwise Rosy would have accidently woke her up.

I can't help but smile at Rosy's retreating back as she goes into Amy's room. I haven't ever smiled this much before, not since Diana and my Father died. Rosy just seems to brighten up my day. God, that sounded so cheesy.

I shut the door as I think about the day ahead of me. Going to the beach with Rosy is going to be great. It's going to be so much fun being able to spend time with Rosy, just one on one without having to worry about anything and without her schooling getting in the way. Not that I mind that, mind you. I will take any chance I get to hold Rosy on my lap and have my hands on her. It's fun seeing her learn, anyway.

Yet again I grin.

(Rosy's POV)

I could barely decide what to wear. One piece or two piece? Pink or blue? I tried to remember everything Amy told me about being a teenage girl.

I finally just pick one. Putting it on in the bathroom, my mind is filled with lots of random thoughts. When I am done I look at myself in the floor length mirror.

I chose a light baby blue two piece. It is just that solid blue colour with frills on the bottom piece. The top piece tied around the back and around my neck. I look nice in it.

Over the top I throw a strapless white dress on that goes to mid-thigh. Next I look at my hair. I brush it as best as I can, but I can't help but think Ashton is better at it. Next I grab a hair band and try to tie my hair up. I frown in frustration when it doesn't work out properly.

I turn and bound out of the room and down the stairs, looking for Ashton's Mum, Linda. I find her in the kitchen, making coffee for her and Ashton.

"Could you please help me tie my hair up?" I ask, stepping up to her.

She smiles at me. "Sure, hair band." She says, holding her hand out. I give it to her and turn around. "Wow," She says, "Your hair is so long."

"Yeah, I guess it is..." I laugh nervously.

Just like Amy, Linda ties my hair up in a high ponytail with a few quick motions. My fringe stays out, which I like.

"Thanks." I smile, sitting on one of the stools at the kitchen bench.

"So what are you and Ashton going to do today?" Linda asks me as the toaster pops.

"He said that we can go to the beach." I grin.

Linda smiles. "Well that sounds fun."

"Yeah. I don't think I've ever been to the beach." I say.

"Really? Can you swim?" She asks with a hint of worry.

I nod. "I think I can. I mean, I can swim in wolf form. There is a lake I used to play in. Plus I remember that at our old house was near a pool and Jack and I used to swim there sometimes." I say.

She nods. "Ok then." She says, sliding toast with peanut butter across at me.

"Thanks." I smile, biting into the toast.

Ashton comes down the stairs in black and blue board shorts and a white shirt. I smile at him, and he smiles back.

Ashton sits on the stool next to him. Linda gives him coffee, and he thanks her.

I listen absentmindedly as the two chat.

When Ashton puts his cup down and turns to talk to his Mum, I steal a sip out of it. It isn't as bad as I first thought it was.

"Ready to go?" Ashton asks a little while later when we both finish eating breakfast and packing the car.

"Yeah." I grin. "Bye Linda!" I wave over my shoulder as I exit the house.

"Bye Mum!" Ashton calls, following me out.

"Have fun you two!" Linda calls after us, smiling.

I can't stop smiling as I sit in the front seat of Ashton's car and pull my seatbelt on. This is going to be fun.

Ashton hops in, pulls his seatbelt on, starts the car and exit's the driveway. His house is out in the forest, so it takes a few minutes to get onto the road.

"So you like coffee now, huh?" He asks, smirking over at me.

I blush. Guess he saw me.

We get to the beach a little while later.

My jaw hits the floor as I look at the beach. It's so beautiful! The sand is a golden white colour, the water a crystal clear blue and green colour and the sun is shining over everything.

"You like it?" Ashton asks, reaching over to brush his fingers over my hand to get my attention.

"It's so pretty!" I exclaim, practically bouncing in my seat.

Ashton grins at me. "Come on, let's go." He says, hopping out with the keys in his hand.

I excitedly hop out and shut the door. I head for the boot, and so does Ashton. I pull out my beach bag that Linda gave me. It has a towel, water, food, sunscreen and sunglasses in it. Ashton has a bag with similar things in it, except he has his keys and a mobile phone too.

I follow Ashton as he leads me across the sand dunes. There are people on the beach our age, and I wonder why. When I ask Ashton he says their school probably had a teacher's strike or something.

We reach a spot on the soft sand and spread out our towels. I am bouncing with excitement. I want to get to the water.

Ashton takes his shirt off and I shimmy out of the dress. I put it in my bag so it doesn't get dirty and pull out the sunscreen. Linda said she doesn't want us getting sunburnt so we have to wear it.

As quickly as I can I put it on and rub it in. "Can you help, Ashton?" I ask, turning away from him. I can't reach my back. I pull my hair around in front of me.

"Sure, no problem." He replies.

I wait for him to finish, before doing the same for him. I really want to get to the water, I can't stop staring at it longingly.

"Ready to go in?" Ashton asks, standing up and stretching. He reaches down a hand and pulls me up.

"Yeah, come on!" I cry, grabbing his hand and tugging him along.

He laughs at my eagerness from behind me. His grip tightens on my hand as he intertwines his fingers with mine.

As we reach the shoreline I tentatively step into the clear water. I yelp happily- the water is so cold!

Ashton smiles down at me and tugs me further in. I scream happily as the water sprays up my legs. Ashton pulls me in again until I am standing thigh deep in the water.

"It's so cold!" I exclaim.

"Don't worry, you'll get used to it." Ashton laughs.

I walk out a little further, letting the water come almost up to my chest. On Ashton it's not as high, and he doesn't seem bothered by the water.

I suddenly have an idea. A large smile comes to my face, making Ashton watch me warily. Before he realises what I am going to do, I throw a wave of water in his face.

As shock comes to him, I burst out laughing.

Ashton shakes the water off him. "Oh, you think that's funny, do you?"

"Yep." I smirk at him.

A moment later I am covered in salty water.

I splutter out a shocked noise. "You so did not just do that." I scowl at Ashton.

"Oh I think I did... twice!" Ashton laughs, splashing me again.

I laugh and splash him back, before ducking away from the next wave he pushes at me. I jump at Ashton, pushing him underwater for a brief moment. He resurfaces, laughing, before pulling me down with him next time.

I submerge under the water with Ashton. Automatically my legs clamp onto his waist and my hands go to his shoulders. I close my eyes so the water doesn't sting them.

For the briefest moment when I am underwater and all I can feel is Ashton holding me, the strangest feeling sparks in my chest. It's like everything stops so I can savour every touch he gives me.

I open my eyes for a second, taking in his appearance, before they close again.

Ashton's eyes are closed too. His thick eyelashes cast small shadows on his face. His dark, pitch black hair is moving softly with the current under the water. His lips are set in a thin line to stop water from getting in his mouth, and look softer than before. They are curled up in a small smile. His cheeks are slightly flushed, as if he were embarrassed about something.

For that brief moment, I feel safe. I feel secure, and I feel... loved. I feel like I belong here, being held by him and him only.

I felt like I never wanted that brief moment to end.

But all too soon it does.

Ashton pushes up off the sand banks and breaks through the water's surface before we both take in a deep breath of air.

Ashton shakes his head, flinging drops of water out of his hair. A grin spreads across his face, making me feel weak at the knees.

That same strange feeling bubbles in my chest again. I blush as I realise I still have my legs clamped to his waist and my hands are still on his shoulders, but I cover it up with a grin as excitement creeps back into my system. His arms are looped under my thighs, his hands linked.

"That was fun." I say.

Ashton grins at me too. "That it was."

Chapter Seventeen

Recap:

I felt like I never wanted that brief moment to end.

But all too soon it does.

Ashton pushes up off the sand banks and breaks through the water's surface before we both take in a deep breath of air.

Ashton shakes his head, flinging drops of water out of his hair. A grin spreads across his face, making me feel weak at the knees.

That same strange feeling bubbles in my chest again. I blush as I realise I still have my legs clamped to his waist and my hands are still on his shoulders, but I cover it up with a grin as excitement creeps back into my system. His arms are looped under my thighs, his hands linked.

"That was fun." I say.

Ashton grins at me too. "That it was."

It is afternoon time now. Ashton and I spent the whole day at the beach, laughing and playing in the water. Luckily neither one of us got sunburnt, that would've hurt.

Right now I am lying stomach first on my towel, watching the sun dip down behind the water's horizon. It made the water seem orange and it is really beautiful.

Ashton was the same.

All throughout the day, whenever he touches me, all I can feel are those sparks. They have seemed bigger, brighter since the thrilling moment when Ashton dragged me underwater and I clung onto him tightly.

I sighed happily, looking at the reflection of the orange sun on the water again. I turn to Ashton. "Want to go for a walk?" I ask hopefully. I really need to move, it feels weird just lying around doing nothing.

Ashton nods. "Sure." He says, standing up. "Come on." He puts a hand down and I take it to haul me up on my feet.

Together we make our way down to the shoreline.

"How come the water is further up on the sand now?" I ask Ashton, splashing some water a little with my bare foot.

"Well, the tides get pulled up by the gravitational force of the moon. So the more the moon rises, the higher the tide is. The further away the moon is, the lower the tide." He explains.

"Oh, well I guess that makes sense." I say.

For a while we settle into a silence, walking side by side but not touching. My left hand constantly brushes against his right one, whether he does it or I do it. It's like both of us are afraid to hold each other's hand in case it might seem to... forward.

But I want to. I like the fact that his hand is so much bigger than mine and is always so warm. It's like he's my personal heater.

With a frustrated little sound and a scowl I reach for his hand and tentatively intertwine our fingers, before smiling to myself. That's better, I think to myself, happier now.

I look back out across the orange sea, a ghost of a smile on my lips as mine and Ashton's hands swing back and forth gently. It's so peaceful out here. The sound of the waves crashing on the shore and the warmth of the sun and Ashton are making me sleepy.

Leisurely we head back to where we placed our towels and pack up. Ashton leads me back to the parking lot where we put our stuff in the car. There is a tap shower sort of thing where we wash the sand off us before drying in the sun quickly.

I yawn as we hop in the car, curling up in the chair. Ashton hops in on the other side and starts the car. He doesn't seem as tired as I am.

Ashton starts the car and drives out of the parking lot. I turn in the seat to face him, resting my head on the chair and close my eyes. Ashton reaches over and holds my hand with one of his.

I yawn and grip onto it tighter, before falling asleep peacefully.

I am barely half awake, still half asleep actually, when Ashton finally stops the car.

He takes his hand away from mine and gently shakes me awake. "Come on angel, we're home." He says.

I groggily wake up, only just able to keep my eyes open. Ashton leans over me and unclips my seatbelt before pushing my door open.

I mumble a tired thanks before I get out. My legs feel heavy and my hair feels stringy. I reek of salt water and I want to sleep for hours.

As fast as I can -which isn't very fast- I get my stuff out of the boot and take it inside with Ashton following behind me. I put my dirty towel and the sundress I wore in the washing machine and the rest of my stuff on the kitchen bench. I'll clean it up in the morning.

Ashton does the same. As we walk up the stairs, I try not to fall on my face, but I'm so tired.

We reach Ashton's room and he nudges me towards his bathroom. "Go have a quick shower then get changed."

I nod, knowing he will shower in the main bathroom.

Doing as he says, I have the quickest shower ever to get the salt and sand off me. It takes a little longer to get the sand out of my hair. I dry myself, then pull my pyjama's on. Linda had left them in here for me in case I needed them. My pyjamas are only purple pyjama pants and a white singlet, but that is comfortable to sleep in.

When I come back out Ashton is already in his bed. It must have been easier to wash off for him because he doesn't have long thick hair.

I really don't want to sleep in my bed, I realise. I had a better night of sleep when I slept in Ashton's bed, especially when it's cold and he is so, so warm.

I stumble to his bed and pull the covers back. Ashton jumps and his eyes fly open as he watches me. I keep quiet and crawl under and over to him. I let the covers fall over me as I squish myself to his chest.

Instantly his arms go around me and pull me closer. "Rosy?" His soft voice greets my ears. "You alright?" He sounds worried.

I mumble something incoherent and rest my head on his strong forearm. "Fine." I manage to finally say, mixed in with a lot of other strange, tired noises. My eyes droop closed as I slump against his hard, bare chest.

Ashton starts rubbing circles on my back through my singlet. "Is everything alright?" He tries again.

"Yeah." I say, but my voice comes out as a dreamy sigh as a nice warmth blossoms through my body, making me sleepier.

"Why are you here?"

I stiffen, suddenly feeling a little more awake. "I'm, uh, err... Sorry..." I mumble, trying to move away from him feeling embarrassed.

Ashton pulls me impossibly closer again. My body gets lined up flush against his, even though he is taller than me, making my face go red. "No, I want you here." He whispers into my hair, burying his face there. He sounds like he wants to say something else, but he keeps it to himself.

Well, I think to myself, this is comforting.

Ashton moves his hand to the back of my head and tucks my face into the crook of his neck. His fingers tangle in my hair. All I can smell is his intoxicating scent, like the forest and something else sweet, but still masculine at the same time.

I nuzzle my face into his throat, breathing in his scent again. Something about Ashton seems different. Something seems... better, if that's possible.

I rest my head on Ashton's bare shoulder. His skin is warm. He settles around my smaller body, tugging me closer again.

I sigh to myself.

A minute or two later, and I finally fall asleep.

In the morning, I don't wake up early like I usually do. In fact, it is Linda that wakes me up.

"Ashton. Rosy. Time to wake up." She says quietly, shaking us both by the shoulder gently.

I groan. "Don't want to." I mumble tiredly, curling back into Ashton's warm chest. His arm tightens around my waist as he presses into my back.

Linda chuckles. "Come on Rosy, breakfast is ready. And Ashton, I know you're awake so get up and get your butt downstairs." She adds in a strict tone.

He groans before slowly slides his arms off of my waist. When I am free I stretch out big like a cat and yawn.

I roll off the bed and yawn again. I follow after Linda as she leads me down the stairs and to the kitchen. Waiting on the bench is a bowl of fruit salad and a glass of orange juice. I feel my eyes light up at the sight of the bright coloured food.

I leap on the stool and start forking down my food like a starving person.

Ashton comes down shortly after and sits next to me on the other stool again. Linda gives him fruit too, as well as coffee again.

I keep my eyes off the coffee this time.

School with Ashton that day was as usual. I was learning quickly, Ashton's says, and I am proud of that. The day ended quicker than I thought it would. I enjoyed it.

In the evening it started raining, so Ashton and I didn't get to go for a run, which bothered me. Amy was with a friend all evening, so I didn't get to talk to her at all. I avoided Jack as much as I could, and ended up escaping to Ashton's room when he got a little too close for comfort. I'm not ready to face him just quite yet. I haven't forgiven him for yelling at me for no reason, even if he was defending his mate. I'm just not ready yet.

I had had a shower and changed into my pyjamas after running from Jack, before crawling into Ashton's bed. Mine seems too small now I've slept in his. It seems to empty without having someone else there to curl up with- meaning Ashton.

Later that night he had finally come to bed. Since it was Tuesday, he brushed my hair before lightly kissing my forehead, making me blush and duck my head. He didn't say anything about me being in his bed, just simply went to have a shower and get changed before crawling under the covers and pulling me against his bare chest.

That night I asked him why he always slept without a shirt.

Ashton said it was because sleeping with a shirt was too uncomfortable. I told him I liked sleeping with a shirt on. He chuckled and said that I am a girl; I have to sleep with something on to cover my 'lady parts', especially when I sleep with him. I said that that makes sense.

Then he had gotten all worried and said that if I didn't feel comfortable with that and still wanted to sleep next to him that he could put a shirt back on.

Then I chuckled and said that I liked him sleeping without a shirt on because he is softer and warmer to cuddle up to.

He chuckled then, and we both went to sleep wrapped up in each other.

All over, it was a happy day.

(Ashton's POV)

When I wake up that morning, it is to a warm feeling spreading across my body. Rosy is arched up in front of me, the both of us on our sides. Her back is pressed against my chest, my arms curled around her slim waist. Her head is resting on my forearm, her hair tumbling down her back in soft, glossy waves.

An utterly peaceful look is over her face. Her mouth is partly opened as she breathes evenly. She has both her arms wrapped around my arm, the one her head rests on. All I can feel is her skin on mine and the sparks that connect the two of us, prove that we are mates. Again I wonder if she can feel them, or if she can't feel them.

The thought of her not feeling the sparks disappoints me.

I pull Rosy's back closer to my chest and rest my head above hers on my pillow. Her scent fills my nose. She smells like soft soap and jasmine, a wonderful scent that makes me feel slightly dizzy- but in a good way.

Rosy mumbles something that I can't quite understand, and softens against my body. She rubs her cheek against my forearm as she finds a more comfortable position. With a tiny irritated look she lets go of my arm and rolls over to face me. She buries her face in my chest, pressing against me, and slips one of her legs in between mine. And with that she settles back down into a peaceful sleep.

I lie there with what I am sure is an open mouth and wide eyes. To say I am surprised is an understatement. The position she put us in feels so, so... natural. And it feels so damn perfect...

Another warm flash rolls over my body, making my face heat up. I can feel every single inch of her beautiful body pressed up against mine. It's really nice to know that her wolf realises we're mates, even if she doesn't quite realise it yet. All she has to do is mature a little more, and soon enough she will realise it.

It's nice seeing her grow up. It makes me feel like I've known her for her entire life, not just a few short weeks. I feel really connected to her already.

I wonder how she feels about me. It's a tormenting thought that could keep me entertained all day but probably would really frustrate me.

I put my arms around her back and drive my fingers up through her silky blonde hair before tightening them around the back of her head. She moans a little pleased sound in her sleep. It makes me smile like a fool.

I rest my head next to hers. Rosy is lower down on the bed than I, so her head is on the bottom of the pillow and her face is facing my chest, currently buried in it. I rest my head on the pillow above hers, since I am higher up on the bed.

It's only now that I realise it's still quite early in the morning. I close my eyes and let sleep wash over me. Again.

Waking up I am in the same position that I went back to sleep in. The only difference is that Rosy moved a little closer again, aligning our bodies parallel with every part of us touching. Again it makes me go red. I never thought that I would be this close up to her this early, even if it is in her sleep. She may not be aware of what she's doing, but I couldn't be happier.

I wonder why my Mum hasn't gotten us up yet. It's a Wednesday, a school day. She usually gets us up. Eh, doesn't matter. She's probably just sleeping in like she should be. I could never understand how she got up so early.

Slowly I unwind my fingers from Rosy's hair and move my arms away from her. She makes a small whimpering noise and pushes into me again.

I move my hand to cup her cheek.

Her expression softens once more.

"Rosy, it's time to wake up." I whisper, thumbing her cheek softly.

Her eyes flutter a little, but she just curls back up to sleep again.

I smile at her sleeping face. She's just so lovable. "Come on Rosy." I nudge her hip with mine gently.

She breathes out heavily, and I know she's awake. "Ashton?" She mumbles weakly, rubbing one of her eyes.

I chuckle at her. "Yes, angel."

"I'm tired."

"We have to get ready for school." I tell her.

She groans, rolling over so her back is facing me. She rests her head on the pillow again, her hands under her hair.

I put my arm around her press my chest into her back. I rest my chin on her thin shoulder. "Come on Rosy. Time to get ready for school." I murmur.

She sighs. "Do I have to?" She mumbles. I wonder why she is suddenly so tired. She usually wakes me up when she sleeps in her bed. But most of the time when she is in my bed she sleeps in like I do, except for the one time when she tackled me off the bed and said I look like a goldfish.

"Sorry, but yes you do." I laugh quietly at her. "But don't worry, I have to too."

She breathes out again. "Fine."

I sit up, pulling Rosy up with me. I keep my arm securely around her slim waist. "Go get dressed, I'll make us breakfast." I say.

She nods her head obediently. Wriggling out of my embrace, I watch her as she hesitantly leaves the room, glancing back at me once. I smile at her reassuringly, and she smiles back before bouncing off down the hallway with a pretty smile on her face.

I can't help but smile at her retreating back; like always.

I get up from under the covers and head to my closet. I get dressed quickly- just a pair of dark blue denim jeans and a white V-neck shirt that kind of sticks to my body.

I suppose it takes longer for girls to get dressed because Rosy usually takes longer than I do. Amy and my Mum take ages to get dressed too.

I decide to just make toast and poached eggs. It's quick and easy and Rosy loves it. I still remember how happy she was when my Mum made them a few days ago.

Upstairs I listen to Rosy's easy breathing. Her breathing, for me, is easy to pick out among a crowd. Her breathing pattern is different to everyone else's. It's nice to listen to her heart when her emotions change.

Just as the toast pops and the eggs finish cooking Rosy comes bounding down the stairs. She's wearing dark blue denim shorts and a white, partially backless shirt.

I chuckle at her.

"What?" She asks insecurely, looking down at herself. "Do I look bad or something?"

"No!" I am quick to assure her. "We match." I say.

She looks at her dark jeans, then to mine, then from my white shirt to hers. Then she starts giggling, making me smile a little. "Yeah, I guess we do match." She says happily, before sitting down on one of the kitchen stools.

She waits patiently as I put the food on a plate and hand it to her, before doing the same for myself. I sit on the stool next to her and start eating. All throughout the meal I look at her out of the corner of my eye, watching her as she focuses on her meal, letting her bright blue eyes wander around the room aimlessly. She always seems so preoccupied yet when you talk to her she snaps to attention as if she was just waiting for someone to speak to.

She's just so, so... amazing.

Chapter Eighteen

Sorry for the long wait, I've been really sick lately :(I'm gonna warn you know, my uploads for all my stories are gonna be pretty screwed up for a while, but if I can find time I'll upload on time again.

Enjoy!!

xox

Recap:

(Ashton's POV)

I chuckle at her.

"What?" She asks insecurely, looking down at herself. "Do I look bad or something?"

"No!" I am quick to assure her. "We match." I say.

She looks at her dark jeans, then to mine, then from my white shirt to hers. Then she starts giggling, making me smile a little. "Yeah, I guess we do match." She says happily, before sitting down on one of the kitchen stools.

She waits patiently as I put the food on a plate and hand it to her, before doing the same for myself. I sit on the stool next to her and start eating. All throughout the meal I look at her out of the corner of my eye, watching her as she focuses on her meal, letting her bright blue eyes wander around the room aimlessly. She always seems so preoccupied yet when you talk to her she snaps to attention as if she was just waiting for someone to speak to.

She's just so, so... amazing.

(Rosy's POV)

I finish the delicious food Ashton made me and stand to put my dish in the sink. I reach over the kitchen bench and take Ashton's dish too, since he's finished eating. I don't really know how to wash up properly, but I have watched Linda do it. I feel like I should help out, so I move the dishes into the dishwasher. I would turn it on if I knew how, but there are so many buttons.

So I end up standing there looking down at the full dishwasher, confused.

Ashton chuckles and stands up. He comes over and stands next to me. He presses a few buttons on the dishwasher.

I try to watch and take in what he does, but it's a bit hard to keep track of what he's doing.

Ashton reaches for my hand and folds my fingers into a fist, except for my index finger. He moves me finger over the start button, which I push. My confused look turns into a smile as the dishwasher starts. Sometimes the smallest things seem so hard, yet with Ashton around they aren't even a little complicated.

"Come on, let's go start school." Ashton smiles down at me, amused.

I nod, starting to feel a little bit brighter. School is fun with him, but sometimes it gives me a headache from trying to take in everything in just one day. I am learning really fast, Ashton says, but every now and then it gets a little bit hard. Sometimes it can get boring, but other times its fun. I like science, but I don't like maths. I like art and music lessons, but we don't do much of that because of the other more important classes, and when we do it's only when I need a short break from learning too much at one time. But I guess it is my fault sometimes when I push Ashton to teach me more, which always makes him laugh and me blush.

I like the werewolf lessons too. Ashton teaches me about mates, and Alpha's, and the werewolf history. He's teaching me to fight and run in wolf form when we run, even if I don't realise it. When we play fight, it's an unintentional way of teaching me to fight, even if he does let me win all the time.

Ashton leads me to the room set up as a classroom. I like it because of the windows that let in a lot of sunlight in the afternoons. It makes the room nice and warm.

My school stuff is spread out on the desk. Everything from workbooks to textbooks to pencils are all in their place. It doesn't look messy, it looks clean and neat.

Ashton sits down on the chair and pulls me onto his lap. The first time he did that because I couldn't write properly and he had to help me, but now it's just natural and comfortable. It's easier for him to monitor what I'm doing if I'm right in front of him, instead of when he's in front of me and sees everything upside down.

I reach forwards and drag my pencil case and a workbook closer. Ashton watches me over my shoulder.

For the next hour or so he teaches me about similes and metaphors, about narratives and recounts and other writing styles. I like English lessons too, they're fun. I love writing now because it's easier and doesn't frustrate me as much. Sometimes I spell stuff wrong, but Ashton always corrects me in a nice way. He is never bossy or strict, always just gently urging or nudging me in the right direction or causally reminding me how to spell something.

Ashton puts his hands on my hips and watches me closely, correcting me when I spell or write something wrong and telling me little things here and there.

It's really nice to have Ashton around.

By the end of the day, my wrist is sore from writing. Letters and numbers keep swimming before my eyes. Ashton made me take a break after lunch which is when I was able to do art, but after that I had to do maths. I hate maths. It's so boring.

Ashton squeezes my hips with his big hands lightly, making me fidget. "We're finished for today, Rosy." He smiles behind me.

I nod, flipping the workbook closed and leaning back against Ashton's hard chest. He tends to be very warm. Subconsciously his arms encircle my waist as his fingers intertwine on my stomach. He rests his chin on my shoulder.

"This is my favourite part of the day." I say, breaking the calm silence. I blink a few times, fighting off a comfortable warm.

"Why?" Ashton asks curiously.

I sweep my hands towards the windows where sunlight streams into the room like golden beams, falling across mine and Ashton's lap but not hitting my face or chest. "Because of the sunlight. It's so warm and calming and I just love it." I tell him.

He smiles against my throat. "I love it too."

I can feel his breath wash does my neck, which makes me shiver. I don't know how to answer that without embarrassing myself, so I stay quiet and settle back against Ashton's chest. I seem to fit right in the curve of his body perfectly, which makes me wonder why that is. I fit on his lap properly, I'm small enough that my head gets tucked under his nicely and his arms always seem to be around my waist comfortably.

He's always with me or around me, always comes when I call for him in wolf form and human form. Every night he lets me sleep in his bed with him and he always holds me in his arms. Now that I think about it, he hardly ever stops touching me in some way. Even during school time he has me on his lap and his arms are around my waist.

And Ashton always cares for me. Whether it is making me lunch -which he always does for me- and other meals, or running with me in wolf form, or holding me when I cry or have a nightmare, he is always there to care for me. No matter what, he's always there for me.

Ashton just seems so perfect to me. He didn't have to save me that night the rogues first attacked, save me twice in fact. He didn't have to give me a home and food. He didn't have to comfort me when I cried or had a nightmare. He didn't have to buy me clothes or a bed or a wardrobe. He didn't have to help me when that rogue approached me at the shopping centre. He didn't have to come after me when Jack yelled at me or when Blake and Tim took me to the veterinary clinic. He didn't have to move my bed into his room or let me sleep with him, he doesn't have to tutor me or go for runs with me. He doesn't have to let me practically walk all over him when I get scared or let me hide behind him when Jack comes around. He doesn't have to do any of that for me.

But he does. He does it all. For me.

But why though? Why is he so nice to me? I have had barely any time to know him, but I feel like I have known him for my entire life. It's the strangest feeling, but I believe that I would be unhappy without him around.

Which makes me wonder. "Ashton, who are you... to me?"

Ashton stiffens all around me. His arms tense around my waist, clinging on to me tighter. I lean back against him and rest my head on his shoulder in an attempt to comfort him. He doesn't relax much, making me frown a little.

"Ashton?"

He lets out a breath he had been holding. "What do you mean, angel?"

I fidget a little again. "You're always so nice to me, and I know you're the alpha but is that why you're nice? Am I just another wolf?" I felt kind of stupid babbling, but I want my question answered.

I feel Ashton shake his head. "You're not just another wolf." He growls.

I nod and he relaxes a little, but not much. "Then who am I to you? And who are you to me?" I ask again.

Ashton stays quiet for a while.

I don't pressure him to answer me, because it might annoy him and then he wouldn't answer at all. If I wait for a minute, he might answer me. It's just about giving him some time to think it over, I suppose.

I feel Ashton breathe out behind me, again his breath washing down my neck and making me shiver a little. He opens his mouth to answer me, but before a single word leaves his lips the classroom door is opened and someone comes in.

I growl a little in frustration. I wanted to know, but now someone has interrupted! I guess I will have to find out later.

Ashton turns his head back to see who the person is while I glare at the windows.

"What?" Ashton asks with a blank voice, keeping his annoyance in check.

"Sorry to interrupt, Alpha, but we have a slight problem." A stranger's voice says.

I turn my head to the other side and look back over Ashton's shoulder to see someone around his age standing there.

"Um, hi." He replies nervously, looking anywhere but me.

"Hi." I say back, looking at Ashton confusedly.

"Rosy, this is Joshua. He's my beta." Ashton says carefully, moving one of his big hands to hold my hip as I twist around to look at Joshua properly. My chest ends up pressing against Ashton's as I struggle to remember what a beta is. Isn't a beta the Alpha's second in command? "Joshua, this is Jack's little sister, Rosalina." Ashton tells Joshua. My full name sounds nice when he says it.

Joshua nods as understanding crosses over his face.

"So what's the problem?" Ashton asks, turning into serious mode. His face holds no sign of amusement or even boredom.

"It's the rogues. They're attacking."

That makes me stiffen as a bucket of icy cold fear gets thrown all over me. I shrink closer to Ashton's chest, making my shirt ride up a bit as I clamp my legs around his waist.

Ashton stiffens too. Both his hands go to my hips, skin on skin since my shirt moved. I feel his nails bite into my flesh, but I don't complain. A low growl rumbles from his chest; I can feel it. I bury my head into the crook o f his neck, fighting back a whimper.

"I'll be there in a moment." Ashton says.

Joshua nods. "The women and children have been put into the lounge room. There are eight wolves stationed close to the house." He says before leaving.

Ashton continues to snarl under his breath. His fingernails dig into my hips again, making me feel... strange.

I whimper quietly, shaking.

That small noise snaps Ashton out of the angry trance he was in. He pulls me closer and rests his head on mine. He's still tense, but he isn't growling anymore. "Angel, I've got to go help my pack."

I whine, my grip around him tightening. I feel tears spring up behind my eyes, not yet falling.

"I know, angel, I know. You have to stay with the other women, who aren't fighting, and the children." Ashton says.

I guess if women want to fight, they can. It makes sense- women may not be as strong as male werewolves but we sure are a lot faster and more evasive.

"You can stay with Mum, yeah? Is that alright?" He continues talking, sounding honestly worried. His arms tighten around me with every word.

I stay silent, though my body is shaking with fear. I don't want him getting hurt. I don't even want him going, but I know he has to protect his pack. He is the Alpha after all. He has responsibilities he can't ignore just for me.

But that thought still doesn't take away that panicked feeling stirring in my chest. My hands clench in Ashton's shirt as I crush myself against his chest. His soft forest-like yet manly scent fills my nose as more tears crowd my eyes.

Ashton stands up, putting his arms under my thighs to hold me up. I bury my head in the crook of his neck, silently crying.

He carries me out of the classroom without a word being said and takes me to the lounge room. I hear women and children crowding the room, and a sudden flash of anxiety hits me. I don't want to leave Ashton; I don't want to be left without him.

Heaps of people start to stare at me as Ashton takes me. I whimper and clamp my legs around his waist tighter, trying to hide in him. He tightens his arms around me, hoisting me up higher with a little jump.

My nails start to dig into the back of Ashton's shoulders as I feel their stares on my back. Ashton lets out a low, threatening growl that I can feel rumbling in his chest.

Everyone stops staring.

Ashton walks to a corner of the room, beckoning Linda over with one hand. Ashton sets me down on the floor gently, untangling my limbs from his. He leans down towards me, crouching on the balls of his feet, and rests his forehead against mine.

I look into his chocolate brown eyes, watching him with my watery blue ones. He looks like he is about to tell me something, then decides against it.

He slowly brings one of his hands up to my face, cupping my cheek in his palm. His slender fingers brush my hair out of my eyes tenderly as he presses his lips against my forehead. The same sparks that are usually there rocket down my body, making me feel warm and secure. Softly he brushes his nose against mine, making a small smile come to my lips.

"Please come back safe. Please." I plead with him, whispering in his ear before he moves his head away from mine.

Ashton kisses my forehead again, letting his lips linger longer than a normal kiss. His thumb strokes my cheek lightly. "I will, angel. I promise I will."

Chapter Nineteen

Recap:

Ashton walks to a corner of the room, beckoning Linda over with one hand. Ashton sets me down on the floor gently, untangling my limbs from his. He leans down towards me, crouching on the balls of his feet, and rests his forehead against mine.

I look into his chocolate brown eyes, watching him with my watery blue ones. He looks like he is about to tell me something, then decides against it.

He slowly brings one of his hands up to my face, cupping my cheek in his palm. His slender fingers brush my hair out of my eyes tenderly as he presses his lips against my forehead. The same sparks that are usually there rocket down my body, making me feel warm and secure. Softly he brushes his nose against mine, making a small smile come to my lips.

"Please come back safe. Please." I plead with him, whispering in his ear before he moves his head away from mine.

Ashton kisses my forehead again, letting his lips linger longer than a normal kiss. His thumb strokes my cheek lightly. "I will, angel. I promise I will."

(Ashton's POV)

My face contorts into a pained expression as I turn and walk away from Rosy. My lips are tingling from touching her skin, even if it was just two small kisses to her forehead.

I hate leaving her like this, I hate leaving her alone. I know my Mum will protect her as best as she can, but I can't help but think I could do it better.

I was so close to telling Rosy she was my mate when Joshua walked in. I wanted to tell her.

But the fact that there are rogues attacking is more important. They are not going to take Rosy away from me, ever. To get to her they have to get through me.

I stalk out of the house, nodding to a couple of the wolves prowling around guarding the pack house with the pregnant, young, elderly and the woman who aren't fighting in it. In my pack, if you are capable of fighting and actually want to do it, then you will be taught. Every wolf knows the basics of fighting and can hold their own, but some prefer to stay with the non-fighters.

When I get into the trees I strip as I walk, and shift into my huge black wolf. My eyes are still brown. I start running faster to where I know the fight is going on.

It's in a clearing, not Rosy's clearing but a much larger one. The smell of dirty fur and blood fills my nose, as well as the smell of my pack.

I start running faster, my eyes switching to molten yellow as rage sets in. Who dares to attack my pack and thinks they can get away with it? My pack is one of the strongest in the country; we are not to be taken lightly.

When I reach the clearing, all I see is wolves fighting everywhere. People I know are being injured or killed, which hurts a lot.

I leap at one of the rogues as he jumps for a smaller wolf from my pack. We collide in mid air with a thumping sound, dropping back to the ground in a tangle of teeth and claws.

I use my greater strength to my advantage as I force him into a lower position, wrapping my jaws around his neck in one fluid and twisting. I pay no attention to the faint snapping sound as I drop the body from my jaws.

The wolf he was about to attack whines quietly at me, before jumping back into the fray.

I do the same, leaping at a wolf with its back to me and clawing down its spine. I lose count of how many wolves I injure or kill, but I stop the rogues from killing my pack as much as I can. I didn't know there were so many of them.

Which makes me wonder. Why are so many rogues banding together? Why do they want Rosalina so much? What did she do wrong?

Can I save her?

It doesn't matter, because I will anyway. No matter how any rogues I have to get through. I will not let my mate get hurt. Rosalina is mine and no one else can have her.

I rip through another rogue as I try to keep the smaller wolves safe. So far there are more rogues dead than my pack, and that is how I want to keep it.

I howl in pain as a rogue wolf tears into my side. I feel the wolf's claws shred my flesh as a satisfied look passes over its face. I collapse as the wolf lunges for my neck, teeth pulling out fur.

In the very distance I hear a very distinctive scream that I know comes from Rosy. Through the mates bond that has started forming she must have felt the burning pain in my side.

Just the thought of her being in any sort of pain has an enraged roar coming from my mouth as I surge to my feet and tear at the rogue's throat. With a gurgling sound it dies, flopping to the ground limply.

I rear up on my hind legs and aim a howl up towards the late afternoon sky. My entire pack copies me, the sound of our howls mixing together to make one loud, intimidating noise.

With a renewed vigour my entire pack launches another attack on the rogues. Within mere minutes more than a dozen rogues have fallen to the ground dead. I tear through wolf after wolf, my only thoughts on Rosy and making sure no one gets to Rosy. I can feel blood dripping down my side and a lot of pain, but I push it away.

Rosy needs to stay safe.

Whatever the cost, I will keep my mate safe.

(Rosy's POV)

I was crying loudly on Linda's shoulder, clinging onto her body tightly. Many of the women, especially the pregnant mates, were crying quieter than me. Some of the children were crying loudly too. I can hear the sounds of the fight in the distance, which is frightening me a lot.

Little whimpers ring around the room as mates feel the pain their partner feels. Children cling to their mothers while the pregnant stick with the elderly who can help them through this stressful time.

I know there are wolves outside of the pack house guarding us, but I can't help but crave for Ashton and for the comfort he gives me. I wonder why that is.

"Shh, honey, everything's going to be fine..." Linda tires to soothe me, but I only cry harder.

When I feel a piercing pain all down my side, I let out a high pitched blood-curdling scream that makes everyone in the room go quiet.

Linda's mouth opens in shock as she looks me over for injury. Her eyes widen as she realises something, before getting a little teary.

In the distance I hear a loud, powerful howl that is soon followed by lots of other howls.

I stop screaming and continue crying, a lot quieter now, my body shaking and trembling. When Jack comes and sits next to Linda, lightly touching my shoulder, I completely forget that I am ignoring him and latch onto him instead. He's strong and muscled and has a masculine feeling, but not anything like Ashton has.

Jack rubs my back gently as he lets me cry on his shoulder.

After a while I run out of tears and end up hiccupping with my eyes squeezed shut. Jack just hugs me tighter. I can only smell his strange scent, which seems to be mixed in with Mandy's. I guess he marked her and completed the mating process. Gross.

I hear a commotion outside, making me whimper in fright.

"It's all right Rosy." Jack whispers. "It's just the pack."

That perks my interest. Women and children are already filing out of the house to see if their family members are alright.

"I've got to go to the hospital to help the other doctors, ok Rosy?" Jack tells me softly. I forgot he was a doctor.

I nod once, sniffing quietly.

Jack lets me go back to Linda. I curl up in her side, whimpering quietly. She kind of smells like Ashton, but he is her son so I guess it's him that smells like her.

"Is he here yet?" I cry inaudibly, hiding my face in the crook of her neck.

"No honey, not yet." She croons, rubbing my back again.

"Can you tell me when?" I ask sadly.

Linda nods.

I sniff again, listening intently outside. If I can't see the doorway and Linda can, she can tell me when Ashton walks through the door. He will come back because he promised. And people don't break promises without good reason, like my parents had. It wasn't their fault they passed away, and I know I will always miss them but I know they loved me and that's that.

Minutes pass and with every second I get more and more worried. He is coming back, right? He promised he would!

I am so wrapped up in my worried thoughts that I don't hear a thing anyone says around me. It's only when Linda shakes me gently do I look at her alarmed. She points over my shoulder. I turn my head back and look over my shoulder.

I see Ashton slowly walking over to Linda and I, only wearing cut-off jeans. He has a bandage wrapped around his torso where there are thin splotches of red showing through. He is clutching his side with one hand, but there is a determined look on his face.

With a soft cry I fly at Ashton, flinging myself at him. He stumbles back a bit as my weight slams into him, but a second later he wraps his free arm around my waist and buries his head in my hair.

I start crying silently again, wrapping my arms around his waist, careful of his wound. I bury my face in the crook of his neck, after standing up on my toes.

Ashton turns me around so I am glued to his side and leads me towards the stairs. I put my arms around him, helping him to walk as best as I can. I watch every part of his body, making sure he doesn't stumble and doesn't trip over anything.

I know there is a worried expression all over my face. I don't want him hurt more than he already is. I worry about him... a lot.

Every now and then Ashton winces, making me cringe. The thought of him being hurt is painful. I don't like it.

"Are you alright?" I ask Ashton anxiously, helping him up the stairs.

He nods. "Fine." He breathes, though I can tell he's lying.

"You're in pain." I whimper.

He shakes his head. "I'm fine, Rosy, don't worry." He tries to assure me.

Now I shake my head, but I keep quiet. I help Ashton to his room, opening the door and shutting it behind us. I lead him to the bed, making him sit down on the edge. His face relaxes a little as he sits, relief gracing his features.

"Wait here." I instruct, going to his draws and rummaging around for something more comfortable than jeans to wear. I find pyjama pants. Does he need a shirt? He said he doesn't like sleeping with a shirt on, so no. No shirt.

I hand the pants to Ashton. "Change." I say, pointing to the bathroom. He nods and does as I say, heading off to the bathroom.

I sit on the edge of the bed and let out a long, nervous sigh. My heart is beating too fast in my chest and a strange, protective, almost possessive feeling is swamping me.

A moment later Ashton comes out, the jeans balled up in his hands. I take them off him and point to the bed. "Rest." I coax.

He nods silently, laying down on the bed and resting his head on the pillow. I sit cross legged in front of him, watching him when his eyes are closed.

"Aren't you going to sleep too?" Ashton asks, opening his eyes.

I shake my head. "Not yet."

He gazes at me for a moment, before reaching over and gripping one of my hands in his. He squeezes once, before closing his eyes again. A moment later, he falls fast asleep with a peaceful expression on his face.

I stare at Ashton, wondering why I deserve someone like him to be on my side, willing to risk his life to stop the rogues from getting me.

I reach over and brush Ashton's black hair off his forehead. It's getting longer now, almost falling into his eyes.

Slowly I untangle my fingers from Ashton's, trying to ignore the sad look on his face.

I walk into the bathroom, strip and shift into my wolf. I'm a little bigger now, around the size of a normal female wolf, not werewolf.

I trot back into the bedroom. Ashton is still fast asleep on the bed, a strange expression on his face. As gently as I can I climb up onto the end of the bed and lie down. I put my head on my paws and face the door.

No one is coming in until Ashton is healed, I decide. He needs his rest.

Soon enough I fall asleep on the end of the bed, still facing the door.

Chapter Twenty

(Rosy's POV)

I hear someone knock on the door, waking me up instantly with my increased senses. I tentatively sniff the air, and when I don't recognise the scent I stiffen, my fur bristling.

I stretch a little, but then I realise my body is being pinned down. I twist my head and shoulders around to see Ashton has switched sides on the bed. His head is up this way now. Ashton's arms are hugging my torso like he hugs his pillow. Actually, his head is resting on me like he is using me as a pillow.

The bandage around his waist is a little more red now, since he is usually a restless sleeper when I don't sleep in his bed.

A small, content sigh comes from Ashton as he nuzzles his face into my fur.

I smile to myself.

"Ashton?" A voice asks, opening the door. I don't recognise the voice.

A girl pops her head in the door, making me growl threateningly. I narrow my eyes a little, shifting around Ashton protectively. He mumbles a small sound that I can't understand much and clutches his hands in my fur tighter.

My tail swishes, the tip brushing against Ashton's shoulder. A small smile passes over his lips, calming me down instantly.

I turn back to the girl, who looks nervous. Even though I am a tiny werewolf, I am still intimidating- especially since I have teeth and claws and she currently has nothing.

"Umm... I'm Crissa, Ashton's doctor." She says.

I put my head back down on my paws in a submissive gesture, still growling a little.

She steps into the room nervously, a first aid kit in her hand. She enters the room and shuts the door behind her quietly so she doesn't wake Ashton up.

Crissa stands next to the bed facing Ashton and opens the first aid kit. "Could you wake him up please?" She asks, looking at me expectantly.

I nod blankly. Rolling over as best as I can with Ashton gripping onto me, I nudge the top of his head with my nose. He stirs a little, but doesn't wake up. I huff, finally managing to turn completely so he is resting against my stomach.

I nudge him again, letting my tongue dart out to lick his temple.

This time he wakes up. Ashton lifts his head up and looks at me, before a lazy grin slips onto his face, making my heart flutter.

My eyes dart to Crissa, making him turn to look that way.

"Hey Crissa." He says, kind of forlornly as if he were sad.

"Wow, there is so much enthusiasm there, Alpha." She rolls her eyes.

I growl warningly, my wolf not liking her tone. Subconsciously I angle my body around Ashton protectively, using my body as a sort of barrier. I put my head back down on the bed, feeling tired and sleep deprived. I didn't get much rest last night- hardly any at all. I was too worried and too hyped up to relax.

Ashton sits up, taking his hands out of my fur.

I let my eyes close, trying to fight off tiredness. It doesn't really work, because a moment later I fall into a rough sleep.

Ashton shakes me awake hours later. I jolt awake with a frightened yelp, cowering almost instantly, only relaxing when Ashton sends me an apologetic smile. He's in jeans now, a fresh bandage wrapped around his side with no shirt on. There isn't much blood staining it, which makes me think the wound is healing fast, since werewolves heal faster than humans do.

Ashton puts clothes in front of me, scratching behind my ear for a moment before turning his back and sitting on the edge of the bed.

I shift back, not feeling any pain when I do anymore. I pull on the clothes, before crawling towards Ashton, tentatively touching his arm before clambering into his lap and burying my head in the crook of his neck, breathing in his masculine scent.

Ashton puts his arms around my waist and hides his face in my hair, breathing in deeply.

"Why do the rogues keep coming here?"

He sighs; his breath swirling down my neck and making me shiver. "Rogues always have a target when they attack, it's never random." He starts, stiffening a little. "They're coming after you."

I tense up all over, fear invading my heart. I cling to Ashton closer, whining.

"They are not coming anywhere near you!" Ashton growls, his eyes turning molten yellow with rage.

I turn my face towards him, moving my hand to his neck trying to calm him down. An angry werewolf is a dangerous werewolf. "Why would they come after me?" I ask as calmly as I can, my voice snapping Ashton out of whatever he was in.

Ashton shakes his head as his eyes go bright brown again. "We don't know. Before the first night I rescued you have you ever come across rogues?" he asks.

I frown a little. "I don't remember. All those years blended into a few days..." I say dejectedly.

Ashton rubs my back. "Don't worry, angel, we'll figure it out." He says comfortingly, nuzzling his nose against my cheek. I giggle, weakly pushing him away. Ashton smiles that dazzling smile at me again, dipping his head back towards mine to press a swift kiss to my cheek. I laugh again as Ashton continues to shower my face, throat and shoulders in sweet kisses. Sparks explode all around my body.

Ashton twists us both around so I am lying under him on the bed. He holds his weight off me by his elbows and knees, before continuing in showering me in kisses. I laugh and giggle the whole way, making a delighted look stick to his face.

Ashton kisses my cheeks lightly as I turn my head to each side. He nuzzles his nose against mine.

I giggle. "What are you doing?" I ask, cocking my head a little as my blue eyes sparkle and I grin happily.

"Playing." He simply replies, grinning that dazzling grin that makes my stomach do flips over and over again.

I giggle again as he kisses the tip of my nose. I turn my head to the side as he aims for my cheek, making his lips land on mine.

Directly on mine.

I stare at Ashton wide eyed and completely shocked as our lips connect. Somewhere in the back of my mind I notice that even though Ashton is a lot bigger than me, our lips fit perfectly together. His brown eyes are wide like mine as surprise flashes across his face.

As soon as our lips had touched, amazing sparks had absolutely exploded all around my body. I wanted more, I was desperate for more. They give me such a good feeling that I was addicted right from the start.

My eyes flutter closed as my body arches off the bed into Ashton. A surprised noise comes from him, followed by a deep groan.

Ashton starts kissing me passionately and I kiss him back. His lips are so soft and so full it's almost unbelievable.

My hands reach up to tangle my fingers in Ashton's pitch black hair. Its silky soft, softer than I thought it would be. I tug on his hair a little, pulling another groan from him that makes me feel warm inside.

Ashton sits up, pulling me up with him without ever breaking contact with my lips. He sits back on his knees and rests me on his thighs, my fingers still gripping his hair.

Ashton puts his arms tight around my waist and drives his fingers up through my long hair so his hands are around the back of my head. Unintentionally a small moaning sound comes from me.

He tugs on my hair as his arms tighten around me and his lips press harder against mine. All those sensations build up and as a wave of heat rolls over me an astounded gasp parts my lips.

Ashton wastes no time in plunging his tongue into my mouth. Another gasp comes from me as his tongue slides across mine and explores my mouth. A brief moment passes as I wrestle for dominance, but him being an alpha and a male I eventually let him win. He growls, pleased, when I do that, making my lips curl up into a smile.

Nothing in my life has ever felt so right. Nothing has ever felt better than sitting here in Ashton's lap with my lips pressed against his. I never thought anything could feel so perfect.

And I want more. Much, much more.

Tentatively I take my hands out of his silky midnight black hair and trail my fingertips down his chest ever so lightly. His bare skin feels hot against my hands, those same sparks increasing and tugging a small moan from my throat. I smile happily again when Ashton moans, his body melting against mine almost heavily. He must like me doing that, making me smile to myself.

Ashton's fingers tighten in my long, blonde hair as he crushes his lips harder to mine in a desperate and oh-so passionate way. He opens and closes both our mouths in complete sync, making my heart flutter a million miles an hour.

Ashton dominates everything about the kiss in a completely male way, from the position we're in to the tempo of our lips as they move together, creating magical sparks that rocket all over my body and make my skin tingle.

Another moan is pulled out from my chest as he presses his lips against mine harder, slipping his tongue into my mouth again.

When I hear a click as the door to our -yes I said our- bedroom is opened, then I hear a shocked gasp, my eyes fly open as I pull away from Ashton, despite his upset little grumble.

I peer up over Ashton's shoulder at the door, only for my face to turn bright red.

Jack is standing there, staring at me and looking furious with his jaw hanging wide open. "What the hell?!" he yells, his fists clenching into balls.

I shrink into Ashton's chest as his arms tighten around me protectively, his muscles standing out in sharp relief. He growls back at Jack. "Don't you dare yell at her!" He snarls protectively, clutching me closer.

I rest my head on his shoulder subconsciously and kind of nervously, staring up at Jack with eyes that are soon becoming watery.

"Then why were you kissing my little sister?!"

Ashton clamps his mouth shut as he tenses, turning to half face Jack.

A sudden urge jumps at my chest, like when my wolf forces me to shift and go for a run. "I was kissing him!" I growl very defensively.

Jack looks at me wide-eyed. "Why would you do that?" he asks doubtfully.

That pulled me up short. "Why are you asking?" I splutter out randomly.

"Because you are my little sister and it is my job to make sure you don't get hurt." He growls.

"Why would Ashton hurt me?" I ask, confused.

Jack just shakes his head at me, leaving the room.

I watch him leave, a heavy feeling settling in my chest. Why wouldn't Jack support my decision? Shouldn't he be glad I'm not acting like a baby anymore? Shouldn't he be glad and happy for me?

I slip my arms around Ashton's waist, hugging him and burying my head in the crook of his neck. Ashton keeps quiet and tightens his arms around my waist, resting his head on the side of mine. It's comforting, to say the least.

My hands clench behind Ashton, my fingernails scraping across his bare skin lightly. I smirk when I feel a shiver run through Ashton's body and his arms tighten around me. I turn my head towards his throat, watching his muscles move up and down as he breathes in and out steadily.

It feels horrible being in a fight with my brother. I might not have known him for more than half my life, but I had a blood connection with him that can't be erased no matter what. I hate fighting with him, even if the reason we're fighting isn't my fault.

I know siblings are supposed to hate each either on the outside, but deep down everyone knows they love each other. They are supposed to support each other, help each other out and give each other good and helpful advice.

Why isn't Jack doing that for me? Did I object when he and Mandy got together, even though they barely knew each other, mates or not? I've known Ashton for ages, he's been with me and comforted me and I really love having him around. I miss him when he's not with me. Isn't that proof enough that I want to be with him? Jack knows him as well, he should be happy for us.

"Why doesn't Jack support me?" I ask, my voice barely a whisper.

Ashton shrugs lightly, not wanting to bump my head too much. "I don't know, angel. Maybe he just wants what's best for you." He sighs.

I frown. "You are what's best for me." I say before I can stop myself. Instantly a bright scarlet blush spreads across my cheeks. "Right?"

Ashton strokes my hair down, nuzzling his face into the crook of his neck. "Right." He confirms in a firm voice, placing a kiss below my ear, this time making me shiver.

"Great." I say, though my voice sounds a bit breathless and breathy.

"Great?"

"Yeah, great." I smile.

It was later at night when there was a small knock on the door. I was asleep -in Ashton's bed of course- and the knock startled me awake. I bolt upright, accidentally waking Ashton up. He bolts upright too, his arms creeping around my waist and a small growl rumbling from his chest. He pulls me half behind him.

"Rosy?" I hear Jack ask from behind the door.

Relief makes my heart flutter. "Coming." I say softly, turning my head to plant a kiss on Ashton's cheek before slipping out of his arms. I know he watches me as I leave the room, I can feel his burning gaze on my back.

I open the door and slip out, shutting it quietly behind me. I face Jack, feeling determination creep up into my chest. "Ashton is right for me." I say quietly, but firmly, looking up at Jack.

Jack looks down at the floor, his hands in his pockets. "Are you sure?" He looks at me worriedly.

I nod.

He sighs. "Are you ready for a relationship, though?"

I think for a moment. "Honestly? No. But... with Ashton everything feels wonderful. He makes me feel safe and secure, like nothing in the world could hurt me. He's always around me and with me, and he does everything for me without asking a single question. He's just so... so perfect."

Jack nods. "If you are happy with him, then I'm happy. I'll support you, Rosy, you're my sister and I love you no matter what." He promises, swooping me up in a crushing hug.

"I love you too." I say, surprised by the sincerity in my voice.

"But if Ashton ever hurts you I'll kill him, Alpha or not!" Jack says louder, aiming his voice at the room. I hear a faint chuckle in reply.

"Thank you Jack."

"No problem Rosy." Jack chuckles, kissing my forehead once. "Now go before he gets impatient." He nudges me back towards the room.

I smile at Jack, waiting a moment as I watch him walk down the hallway and into his room back to Mandy, his mate, before going back into mine and Ashton's room.

It's dark in the room, because it's around one or two in the morning. I wonder why Jack was up so late. Probably couldn't sleep. Had too much on his mind.

As soon as the door clicks shut behind me and I turn to the darkness of the room, I sense movement in front of me. A moment later I am pinned up against the door, my hands up by my head. I feel someone's hot breath on my neck, before a pair of soft lips kisses the soft spot behind my ear.

My knees start wobbling as a breathy sigh of content escapes my lips.

Ashton smiles against my throat. "And just so you know, you're perfect too."

*

Ok, sorry about the long wait! I was very busy, and it is my school holidays so I'm making the most of the 2 weeks of freedom I have :)

Question- have any of you guys heard of Vocaloids? There's 2 of them on the video of the side! Warning though, it is japanese so most of you probably won't like them, but I think they're adorable :) There are heaps of them! Have a look if you want.

Comment!

:)

Chapter Twenty-One

Recap:

(Rosy's POV)

I smile at Jack, waiting a moment as I watch him walk down the hallway and into his room back to Mandy, his mate, before going back into mine and Ashton's room.

It's dark in the room, because it's around one or two in the morning. I wonder why Jack was up so late. Probably couldn't sleep. Had too much on his mind.

As soon as the door clicks shut behind me and I turn to the darkness of the room, I sense movement in front of me. A moment later I am pinned up against the door, my hands up by my head. I feel someone's hot breath on my neck, before a pair of soft lips kisses the soft spot behind my ear.

My knees start wobbling as a breathy sigh of content escapes my lips.

Ashton smiles against my throat. "And just so you know, you're perfect too."

(Ashton's POV)

An insane blush spreads across my little mate's face, and even in the near pitch black I can see it. It's so damn adorable. Scarlet is soon becoming my favourite colour on her. But then again, I like everything on her. She's beautiful. It's as simple as that.

I let go of Rosy's hands that I had pinned up by her head and slip my arms around her waist. She's not as skinny as she was when she first came here, and I'm glad about that. In my opinion she might need a little more weight on her, but that may be my wolf thinking she needs to be healthy.

I move my hands down to the backs of Rosy's thighs and lift her legs up around my waist. She squeals, making me chuckle quietly, but then she buries her head in the crook of my neck, making me sigh in content.

I carry Rosy back to our bed, loving that I can call it that. Our bed. Ours. I pull the covers back and lay Rosy down gently. For a moment I just gaze at her while she stares at me. Her baby blue eyes seem brighter than they usually are. Her very long, honey blonde hair is all messy from a restful sleep, making her look more amazing than ever, in my eyes. A deep red blush makes its way across her cheeks, settling and standing out.

A slow grin curls up my lips as I gaze down at her.

Rosy gives me one of her half nervous smiles, her arms reaching out for me in the dark.

Without hesitation I go straight to her, curling her into my arms against my bare chest again. She puts her arms around my torso, avoiding the bandage. I move my hand to unwrap the uncomfortable thing, missing the feel of her body against mine without any barriers. Well, besides all of her clothes of course.

I toss the used bandage on the floor before hugging Rosy closer again. For a moment she hesitates, staring down at the faint scars on my side. I watch her as she reaches out and traces the fading marks, making me shiver as her fingers brush over the sensitive skin.

"I felt this." Her soft voice whispers in the dark.

I stare at her, shocked. "Is that why you screamed?" I ask.

She nods. "It was painful. It hurt too much. I started crying." She states quietly, running her fingers over the marks on my side.

I reach towards her and lift the singlet up over her side. There isn't any mark there, so I let her top fall back down. I pull her closer and bury my head in her silky soft hair. Her soft, sweet scent invades my senses and I greedily breathe it in.

"I'm sorry." I say, upset. "I didn't mean to hurt you. I was supposed to be protecting you."

She shakes her head a little. "You were." She says softly.

I frown.

"Don't frown." She whispers, looking up at me intently. She reaches up and brushes her fingertips over my lips. "You did protect me." She praises.

A small smile comes to my lips now. I dip my head down and kiss Rosy's forehead, making me shiver at the sensation of those sparks hitting me, like always when I touch her. A small noise of disapproval comes from Rosy as she grabs my shoulders and lifts herself up to my eyes level, before crushing her lips to mine.

I stare at her, shocked, for a moment before eagerly returning her affections. I tighten my hold on Rosy, never wanting to let go of her, only wanting to be with her forever. I nip her bottom lip lightly, asking for entrance. She waits a moment, before opening her mouth and letting me in.

Kissing Rosy is the best thing I have ever felt before. The way her body fits into the crevice of mine so perfectly because she's so small, the way her soft lips feel even softer than they look, the way her tongue battles against mine for dominance but she always lets me win. I've never kissed anyone they way I kiss Rosy.

A lustful little moan springs from Rosy's throat, vibrating into my mouth. I can feel that sound from my toes to the back of my throat. It makes my 'friend' spring to life, so I move the bottom half of my body away from Rosy's so I don't freak her out. I've barely just got her all to myself, I don't want to ruin it by scaring her.

Rosy whimpers at the loss of half the contact we shared. She slides her body across the mattress and presses her hips and knees against mine. She slips a leg in between mine. I don't think she notices the bulge in my pants, so I continue kissing her like there is no tomorrow.

Her soft lips move against mine in perfect harmony. Her glorious body presses against every inch of mine again. All I can smell is her and her soft jasmine scent. Everything about her captivates me, intrigues me, and makes me need to know more - to know everything about her.

Both Rosy and I pull away at the same time to breathe. I lean my forehead against hers, waiting for her eyes to open once again. Her face is flushed with colour, and when her eyes open I see they are a bright icy blue, sparkling too. Almost the exact colour of the lightest sky.

I grin down at her, my mate, happy beyond belief.

She grins back up at me, a dazzling smile that has my breath leaving my lungs.

I curl her up in my arms again. She rests her cheek on the arm I slip under her head, while I wrap my other arm around her waist and pull her closer.

Rosy reaches over and places her hand on the marks on my side lightly. I sigh in content as her fingers brush over the sensitive skin, offering fiery sparks that jolt around my body. I dip my head forwards again and kiss her forehead, before snaking my hand up to brace the back of her head as I hug her closer.

Rosy nuzzles her face in the crook of my neck, sighing in what sounds like content. "Goodnight, Ashton." She mumbles. I can feel her lips move against my neck as she speaks.

"Goodnight, angel." I kiss her temple, before resting my head on the pillow and closing my eyes.

Just feeling Rosy safe in my arms puts me into that space between sleep and consciousness. I wait another minute, until Rosy's body relaxes and her breathing evens out, before letting myself follow her into sleep.

(Rosy's POV)

When I wake up, I don't feel like moving. All I can feel are those sparks. Those strong arms that I know all too well. That familiar, comforting heat that is all around me. That enticing, masculine scent is all I can smell and is all I want to ever smell.

A satisfied sigh escapes my throat as I nuzzle down into Ashton's warm body. His arm around my waist subconsciously tightens around me and the arm under my head with the hand twined in my hair tightens too.

He takes a deep breath in his sleep, letting it out slowly before curling around me again.

I smile to myself, resting my head on his forearm near his shoulder. I nudge Ashton with my hip, hoping to wake him up.

He just simply grumbles something, nuzzling his face into my hair affectionately. I almost give up right then and there, but I tell myself not to.

I sit and think for a moment. How should I wake him up? Hmm...

As an idea pops into my head I grin. I lean forwards and lightly brush my lips against his. Those fiery sparks rocket down my body again.

I watch as Ashton's eyes fly open, before he leans forwards for a deeper kiss and tightens his arms around me.

But I pull away as soon as his eyes open. He growls a small, demanding growl and leans forwards to finish the kiss. A small kiss doesn't seem like enough to either of us.

I giggle at his frustrated expression when I turn my head away.

In a flash I slip out of his arms, before darting out of the room laughing.

Ashton catches on pretty quickly, and gets up to chase after me. "Rosalina!" He taunts in a playful voice.

I scream in delight as he gets closer to me, probably waking up the whole house. As I bound down the stairs and race into the kitchen, Ashton grabs me from behind and picks me up off my feet, twirling me around. A bubbling laugh comes from me and echoes around the kitchen.

Ashton places me back on my feet and turns me around before effectively crushing his lips to mine persistently. He nips my bottom lip lightly with a small growl, demanding entrance. I don't let him in, just for fun. He makes me smile when he growls, frustrated, his hands tightening on my hips. So I let him in and he grins, which makes me smile too.

"Try and keep it PG, Ashton." A familiar voice chuckles behind me.

I jump, pulling my lips away from Ashton as a deep crimson blush covers my cheeks. When he notices he chuckles silently, caressing down my cheek with the back of his hand. One of his arms is still curled around my waist, and it's now I realise my hands are intertwined in Ashton's silky soft black hair. I take my hands out of his hair and slide them down his still naked chest, before hugging him. I bury my face in his chest to hide my intense blush.

I can't believe Ashton's Mum just saw me kissing her son.

Wait. Isn't she surprised I'm with Ashton? Has someone already told her? I don't see how, I wasn't with him until last night and Jack didn't know until early in the morning... or was it late at night? I'm not so sure anymore.

As if Linda hears my thoughts, she smiles a full blown grin at me. "Oh, I knew it was going to happen sooner or later, dear."

I cock my head to the side a little, which makes Ashton chuckle. I turn in his arms to lean my back against his chest. He slips both his arms around my waist and rests his chin on top of my head. I know he's smiling like a fool.

"What do you mean by that?" I ask, clearly confused and puzzled.

Linda chuckles. "Honey, it's a mother's instinct."

Ok, that's just confuses me even more. My brow puckers as I frown, trying to work it out all in my head.

"So do you two want some breakfast?" Linda asks, moving around in the kitchen still in her pyjamas and fuzzy pink slippers. I can't complain, I'm still in my pyjamas- which are just a white singlet and purple pyjama pants. Ashton is just in pyjama pants.

I think it's going to be a lazy day today.

"Sure." Ashton smiles, leading me towards the kitchen bench.

I move with him absentmindedly, still trying to figure out what Linda meant. How could she have known I would get together with her son eventually? I am just so confused right now.

Sitting down on a stool, I dully note that Ashton pulls the other stool closer to me and curls his arm around my waist again, his hand splaying put on my hip as his fingertips dig into my skin just lightly. I squish closer to Ashton's heated side.

"I don't get it." I finally shake my head at no one in particular.

Ashton chuckles. "Let it go, angel." He whispers in my ear as he leans over closer to me.

I shiver as his warm breath swirls down my neck. I pout at him, sticking my bottom lip out. So he leans down and kisses me, flicking his tongue across my lower lip. I moan quietly enough that Linda won't hear me.

"Hey! That is not a sight I want to see first thing in the morning!" Another voice half growls half yells from behind me.

I sigh as I pull away from Ashton again, despite another one of his frustrated growls. "Can't I kiss her without an interruption this morning?" He grumbles, pulling my closer. I rest my head on his shoulder comfortably.

Jack chuckles. "Mmm... no." He says.

Mandy whacks his arm. "Jack!" She scolds.

He pulls her to his side and kisses her forehead with a loving smile. Surprisingly, it is the same smile Ashton always gives me, which makes me wonder.

Jack and Mandy sit across from Ashton and me, chatting easily with Linda and Ashton as I sit and listen quietly.

I'm still so confused.

"So, are you going to join this pack Rosy?" Mandy asks.

I jump at the sound of my name, completely missing the question she asked. "Huh?"

She laughs quietly, shaking her head once. "I asked you if you were going to join the pack. You're still classed as a rogue." She tells me.

I shrug. "I will... if I'm allowed?" I ask, looking up at Ashton.

His whole demeanour lightens up as if he were a little kid on Christmas day. He is practically glowing. He frantically nods his head, brown eyes blazing. "Of course you can." He smiles his special dazzling grin at me, reaching a hand up to cup my cheek, stroking it softly with his thumb.

I grin back at him, happy too. I turn back towards Mandy and Jack, though Ashton slips his other arm around my waist so his hands link at my hip.

Linda places a few plates full of food and a jug of orange juice on the table, though she gives Ashton a cup of coffee.

Handing out plates to everyone, Linda tells everyone to dig in. No one waits for further persuasion as everyone fills their plates with food, including me. Linda drags a chair in from the dining table and sits at the kitchen bench with us.

"So when can I join your pack?" I ask Ashton after a finish a mouthful of food.

He openly gazes at me. "Whenever you want to, I don't really mind." He tells me, taking a sip of his coffee, trying unsuccessfully to hide his grin.

"Wow, eager much?" Jack chuckles at him.

I blush a light red colour. To be honest, I don't know why I am so eager to join Ashton's pack, and I don't know why Ashton is so eager for me to join. I don't like the idea of being a rogue wolf at all, and I want to experience the comfort of a pack. His pack. I don't know why I feel like I want to be with him so much, it's just a really strong urge I have. I want to be in his pack. With him.

Ashton on the other hand, looks about ready to burst with joy. There is an immensely proud look in his eyes making them sparkle way more than usual, brighter against his dark black hair. "I don't mind her eagerness." Ashton grins at me.

I blush a slightly darker red at his gaze.

Everyone goes back to eating while I stare at Ashton's coffee. My hand creeps across the table as I attempt to steal some like I always end up doing. Ashton sees me out of the corner of his eye and while still talking to Jack about something he nudges the cup over towards me with his fingers.

I grin and take a long drink of it, feeling the strange smoky taste slide over my tongue. I don't know why I keep stealing sips of Ashton's coffee, it just tastes... addictive.

I listen absentmindedly as everyone chats around me.

It's nice to be just around people and not have to think about anything but where the conversation is going to lead to.

After breakfast Ashton kisses my cheek and goes to set up the classroom while I help clean up the kitchen with Linda. Mandy and Jack are already off heading for work.

"So how exactly did you know...?" I ask Linda, still confused.

"I just know, honey." She chuckles.

I clamp my mouth shut in frustration. It's annoying not knowing anything. I would rather know than not know. "That doesn't explain much." I complain, loading dishes in the dishwasher.

"No whining, you're not a child anymore." Linda scolds lightly.

"Sorry." I mumble, pouting guiltily.

Linda ruffles my hair as she shuts the dishwasher. I give her a small smile as I say goodbye and head for the room set up as a classroom where Ashton is waiting.

I close the door behind me as I enter for privacy and look at the desk. Ugh. Maths. I frown as I walk up to Ashton and sit on his lap.

"You don't like maths much, do you?" He chuckles as his arms slip around my waist and he pulls me closer.

I shake my head. "Math sucks. It's too hard." I groan.

Ashton chuckles. "I know, angel. I never liked maths. But it gets easier, I promise."

"Do I have to do it?"

"Yes you do." He says firmly. "Maths is important."

I sigh and lean forwards to drag my grid workbook and maths textbook forwards. Math's really is a pain in my head.

It was an hour and a half later when Ashton finally let me shut the text book. "So what's next?" I ask.

"Whatever you want." Ashton smiles, resting his chin on my shoulder.

"I don't mind." I grin.

Ashton chuckles and pulls my English workbook over. I enjoy English, it's actually quite relaxing. Ashton has even got me reading a book in my spare time for novel study, then asks me questions to write answers to.

"So," Ashton starts.

I raise an eyebrow back at him.

"Every week my pack has a bonfire where we all gather together." He tells me.

I frown. "I didn't know that. You haven't been going. Why?" I ask.

His arms squeeze my waist. "I had you to look after. I couldn't just leave you here, even with Jack. I wasn't ready to do that."

I give him a strange look.

He shrugs. "Anyway. Since today is Friday, tomorrow is the bonfire and I wanted to see if you wanted to go with me?" He asks nervously.

A smile comes to my face. "I would love to! Maybe I could meet some of your pack." I chirp happily.

Ashton grins and kisses the side of my neck. "Great."

"Great?"

"Yeah, great." He smiles.

*

Ok, you should have figured it out by now that I've been doing some editing via my iPod, so everytime I correct a mistake it says I've uploaded.... I HAVEN'T!

Until now of course :)

For those of you you read Bound To Be Mates, that's gonna be uploaded today to, and I have to tell you I really, really, really, really love the new chapter.

I don't know... I just love it!!! So if you do read it, keep an eye out!Please comment! :)

Chapter Twenty-Two

After school I was with Amy when I brought up the fact that I am going to the bonfire with her brother tomorrow.

"What? Since when were you and him together?!" She exclaims.

"Um..."

Amy sighs. "Well you should at least tell me the details. Have you kissed him yet?" She asks.

I nod, blushing.

"Great." She grins at me.

I smile too. "Are you going to the bonfire?" I ask.

"Of course." She rolls her eyes.

"Can you help me get ready tomorrow?" I ask her next, widening my eyes into a puppy dog expression.

She groans. "You know I can't resist." She sighs. "Fine."

I grin, a bubbly feeling popping up in my chest.

"So is this, like, a date?" Amy asks, leaning forwards on her bed.

I blush, but frown in confusion. "I don't think so." I sigh, utterly confused.

Amy sighs. "Well then, we're gonna have to get him to ask you on a date." She grins mischievously.

I cock my head to the side a little. "What are you thinking? Aren't you freaked out that I am going out with your big brother?"

She shakes her head. "No, I'm not like that. I knew it was going to happen sooner or later, I just expected it to come sooner." She admits.

"Why?"

Now she gives me a confused look, before laughing. "Oh honey it's so obvious he's had his eye on you since he first saw you." She giggles.

I blush. "He has?" I ask, secretly happy beyond belief.

She nods her head enthusiastically. "Yeah! He's always so protective of you. When I was first hearing about you from Jack and Ashton, I asked what you looked like and you know what he said? Beautiful. He said beautiful, and wouldn't say anything else." She gushes.

I blush bright red again. "Really?" I mumble, a small smile playing on my lips.

"Yeah!" She exclaims again. "I couldn't believe it! My arrogant, cocky brother was saying a girl is beautiful! He's never even been interested in a girl before!"

That thought alone makes me smile.

That evening after dinner and showers, I was lying on my bed when Ashton came walking out of the en suite. He was rubbing a towel through his glistening black hair, just wearing a pair of pyjama pants.

He smiles at me, throwing the towel back in the bathroom.

I smile back.

He walks over to me and scoops me up, carrying me bridal style. Instinctively I wrap my arms around his neck and bury my face in the crook of his neck, taking in his delicious scent.

He carries me to our bed. I don't bother sleeping in mine anymore; I have to be with him physically now to sleep properly. Without Ashton I can't fall asleep peacefully anymore.

Pulling the covers up over our bodies, Ashton kisses my forehead and mumbles a goodnight. I do the same, burying my head at the base of his neck and inhaling his intoxicating scent again. He smells so addictive.

When I finally wake up I am still wrapped in Ashton's arms, my chest pressed against his. His warmth wraps around me, making me feel comfortable and safe. I can feel those electrifying sparks jumping from his skin to mine, making me smile a little to myself.

He presses his lips to my forehead.

I look up, confused. "You're awake?"

His brown eyes twinkle with amusement.

"For how long?" I ask, a little disappointed he didn't wake me up too.

"A while. I like watching you sleep." He admits, hugging me closer. I bury my head in the crook of his neck to hide my insane blush. That's so sweet of him, but I can't help but wonder why he likes watching me sleep. I decide not to ask him, not wanting to ruin the moment. Besides, I kind of like the idea of him watching me sleep, it makes me feel protected.

Thoughts of what Amy told me yesterday jumble in my mind, making me smile happily. It's nice to know I'm the first girl Ashton has taken an interest in. It makes me feel special. He's the first guy I've ever taken an interest in, obviously. He was my first kiss, too. I wonder if I was his, but I suppose not. He must have at least kissed another girl before. But that thought makes me frown.

"What are you thinking about, angel?" Ashton murmurs curiously into my hair, nuzzling his face on the top of my head.

"Nothing." I say quickly, blushing furiously again.

He chuckles. "I can tell when you lie, Rosy. You're heartbeat picks up." He tells me matter-of-factly. "What were you thinking about?" He asks me again.

"Just how you... were my first kiss and I was just wondering... you know?" I say, rolling my wrist absentmindedly, looking up at his amused face before looking away again with a bright red face.

He chuckles, pulling me impossibly closer and resting his chin on top of my head. "You weren't mine...but you're the only one I've cared about." He tells me.

No matter how hard I try, I can't help that warm feeling bubbling in my chest as I wait for Ashton to continue talking.

"I never had much time for girls." He shrugs when he sees I'm not going to say a thing until he does. "I was busy learning Alpha duties, and then I had to become Alpha at a younger age than usual and I was just... too busy to really get in a relationship." He explains, shrugging lightly.

I never thought about it that way. Ashton did have to grow up quickly when his Dad and sister were killed by the rogues. He has to lead an entire pack and keep everyone in line. It must have been hard on him not to be able to do what other teenagers were doing.

I look at him, smiling like crazy.

He laughs quietly, before dipping his head and pressing his lips against mine. The reaction is immediate, like always. Those sparks that slam into me make my eyes shut in pure bliss. My body arches into Ashton's as my arms wind around his neck, fingers tangling in his hair.

A smile tugs at my lips, which makes Ashton smile too.

Pulling back I bury my head in the crook of his neck again, leaving my arms around his neck. "The bonfire's tonight." I say casually.

He shivers as my breath hits his bare skin. "Yeah."

I can hear the excitement in his voice. "Can I join your pack tonight?" I ask uncertainly, looking up at him with my pleading blue eyes.

He stares at me, surprised, and for a moment I worry he will say no, but when his dazzling grin appears I know tonight is the night.

Later that day, around five at night, Amy was helping me get ready. I've had a shower already, and my hair is almost dry.

Amy chose something for me to wear. Nothing too fancy, nothing too causal. I'm in denim coloured dress, though it's not made of denim. It is layered from my waist down. Above my waist it is simply white with little cropped sleeves.

Amy pinned my hair back after curling it so it falls in soft ringlets down my back. I refused to wear make-up. I'm wearing a pair of white ballet flats with little bows on the top, which suite the dress nicely.

After one final tug, Amy stands back and lets her eyes roll over my hair. I see her smile in the mirror in front of me.

"Thank you, Amy." I say, turning my head back to smile at her.

She smiles at me. "No problem. Now, let's go."

I follow after Amy as we leave her room. I know my way around Ashton's house pretty well, now. Amy goes down the stairs first, heading over to her friends who are waiting in the lounge room.

I head down a moment after her, after telling myself that no one is going to stare. I can't remember when I last wore a dress. I've been a bit too thin to fill one in nicely.

I descend the stares, a thoughtful expression on my face. I walk into a room full of people who are ready to go to the bonfire. My eyes search the room, looking for the brown irises I'm so used to. I see Jack first, with his arm around Mandy's shoulders.

Then I see Ashton, talking and smiling with his pack members. His attention wavers as I step into the room, and he turns and spots me. His special, dazzling smile crosses his face. He politely excuses himself and starts walking towards me, wading through the crowd.

Ashton wraps his arms around my waist and pulls me to his chest. "You look stunning , angel." He murmurs, nuzzling his face into my hair.

I smile as colour rises in my cheeks. "Thank you."

I feel Ashton smiles into my hair. "Ready to go?"

I nod against his chest, still smiling to myself. Ashton lets me go and takes my hand, leading me out with everyone else. There are cars parked out the front, and people are slowly getting into them. I see Amy get into one with her friends, as well as Jack and Mandy getting into another.

Ashton and I go in a car by ourselves. I sit in the front passenger seat, considering I can't drive.

Ashton starts the car and follows another out of his driveway. He holds my hand in his as he drives, and I don't complain. My hand looks tiny in his, but it makes me feel comforted.

"So where exactly is the bonfire held?"

"In the forest." Ashton says without taking his eyes off the road. His thumb draws small patterns on my hand. "The land is owned by my family, so no humans can get onto it. It's especially for my pack, and the bonfires we have."

I nod. "I suppose that's a good idea."

Ashton's lips twitch up a little. He follows a car as it turns down a track I would have never noticed if we were driving past. The tar road disappears and is replaced by dirt. The track is rough, but not too rough. I watch the trees roll past, just smudges of green and brown.

A few minutes later and we arrive in a parking lot of sorts. It's a fairly large clearing in front of a stream, where cars can be parked and left. Aston pulls into a spare spot and stops the car.

"Ready to go?" He asks, turning to face me with a smile on his face.

"Yep." I grin excitedly. I wonder what the people in Ashton's pack are like. I think it'll be nice to be around a large number of werewolves for once.

Hopping out of the car, I notice the car Jack and Mandy rode in arrive. I wave at them as they walk closer, drawing their attention to me. Jack leads Mandy over, holding her hand.

"Hey Rosy." Jack grins down at me, kissing my forehead gently.

"Hi!"

"Are you excited?" Jack questions.

"Yeah! It's gonna be fun."

"Are you going to be alright around so many werewolves?" Jack asks, a worried look coming to his face. Mandy squeezes his hand.

"I should be fine. Right?" I say, a hint of doubt creeping into my voice as I turn my head up to look at Ashton.

He slips an arm around my waist and side-hugs me. "You'll be fine." He reassures.

I return to my smiling self. "Let's go then!"

Everyone laughs at my enthusiastic nature, making light colour come to my cheeks. Ashton grabs my hand and leads me down a path through the trees, parallel to the stream. Up ahead I hear the sounds of a lot of people talking, and I smell their scents. I practically bounce with energy as we arrive at the large, open space.

There are at least a hundred people flittering about. At one end of the field is a marquee of sorts, barbeques set up and smoking. The smell of food washes up my nose. Lined up on tables under the shelter are places of bread, sauces and side dishes.

Three fairly large bonfires litter the field. The space for them had been cleaned away of grass and replaced with sand so there is no chance of anything catching fire. Logs surround the flames, providing a place to sit. Some people brought fold-out chairs and are sitting on them too.

On another side of the field there are guys probably Ashton's age playing footy. People are sitting on the side-lines, watching. Little kids are playing hide-and-seek and tag around the forest edge, laughing and screaming in joy. Groups of girls are sitting in their little circles, doing various things. There are even people running around in wolf form, playing around and barking happily.

"Ashton!" A partially familiar voice calls out. A guy with brown hair approaches Ashton with a few others, smiling.

"Hey!" Ashton calls out, grinning. "Rosy, you remember Joshua here. He's my Beta."

"Oh, yeah! Hi!"

"Hey, Rosy." Joshua says, smiling. He shakes my hand. "How's it going?"

"Good." I grin.

"This is your first bonfire, right?"

"Yep!"

"Well, I hope you enjoy yourself." Joshua smiles, before continuing with talking about guy stuff to Ashton.

I look around, and spot Amy with a bunch of her friends. She catches my eye, and excitedly beckons me over. I tug on Ashton's hand, bringing his attention back to me. "I'm going to go talk with Amy, ok?" I ask, blinking my eyes innocently.

Ashton smiles down at me softly. "Ok, but find me at around seven, ok?"

I nod. Ashton swoops down and kisses my cheek gently, making my face flame up. I let go of his hand and walk away, heading in Amy's direction. She greets me warmly, and introduces me to her friends. Somehow I believe this is going to be a fun night.

Chapter Twenty-Three

After a while Amy and I go to the barbeque station to get some dinner. It's now almost seven o' clock, which means I have to go find Ashton. I wonder why.

We pick up paper plates and get a roll. The man behind the barbeque wearing a white apron smiles at us before putting a sausage on our rolls, nodding. We both say thanks before moving to get sauce and Amy gets cooked onion too. I don't really like onion, so I just have tomato sauce on mine.

We sit down around one of the three bonfires that are now roaring. I can feel the heat radiating off it from metres away. It's surprisingly nice.

Amy and I sit down on a spare space on one of the logs around the fire. I stretch my les out in front of me and start eating slowly, smiling at the delicious flavour. It's nicer than I thought it would be.

"So are you enjoying yourself?" Amy asks.

I nod, grinning.

Amy grins to. "That's good to know. Ashton will be happy."

I smile on the inside when hearing that. "He said he wants me to go find him at seven. Do you know why?" I ask.

She shrugs. "No idea. It's almost seven now. Want to go find him?"

I nod. "Ok, talk to you later." I say smiling, before standing up and wandering off to find Ashton, carrying my plate with me.

It doesn't take me long to find him. His intoxicating scent is easy to pin point, and I start to follow it. Eventually I find him talking to Joshua away from the groups of people. They seem to be discussing something important, and Ashton looks excited.

As soon as I break away from the crowds of people around one of the fires, Ashton turns his head to look at me. One of those cute smiles dances across his face, lighting up his features. He politely excuses himself from Joshua, who just smiles and claps him on the shoulder. A moment later and he has me wrapped up in his arms and his lips pressed against my forehead. A giggle escapes my lips.

"So why did you want me to find you?"

"Well aren't we a curious little kitten." Ashton laughs, his arm around my waist as he leads me back into the main area. "You'll just have to wait a little longer."

I pout up at him.

He just laughs and kisses my temple gently. "It's a surprise."

"But I don't like surprises..."

"Don't worry, you'll like this one." He grins at me.

I roll my eyes. Guess I'll just have to wait then, not that I want to. I really don't like surprises; the suspense makes me feel weird. I like knowing what's going to happen and when. Having more structure in my life really is something I prefer.

Ashton leads me back to one of the fires. He lets me finish eating, though I let him have half of the roll seeing as I got full pretty quickly.

"Ok, you just wait here." Ashton says, that excited smile lighting his face up again.

I cock my head to the side, a questioning look on my face.

He just stands and smiles, kissing my head one last time before wading through the crowd again. Once he is in the free space behind the bonfire I'm in front of, he puts two fingers in his mouth and lets out a whistle. Almost immediately everyone's attention turns to him as the chatter dies down.

"Ok, welcome everyone! I'm sorry for not attending the last few bonfires, but I had some things I needed to do." Ashton smiles at the group of people all looking at him.

Some people give him knowing little smiles, and I wonder why.

"As some of you might already know, we have a guest on our territory." Ashton continues. "All of you know one of our finest pack doctors, Jack, and all of you know his back story."

When Ashton beckons Jack forwards, he walks up with a slightly tight smile on his face. Mandy follows him, her hand in his. I can tell she reassures him.

"It seems like Jack has found his mate, Mandy." Ashton smiles, clapping him on the back. "But not only has Jack found Mandy, but he's found someone else."

I watch, slightly confused as Ashton makes his way over to me. The crowd parts for him.

"Everyone, this is Rosalina. She is Jack's little sister. I would like for you all to welcome her." Ashton smiles, wrapping an arm around my waist.

Everyone turns to look at me, and I suddenly feel a wave of warmth flood my cheeks.

The next hour flew by in a mixture of greetings, hugs, cheek pinching, and kisses on the forehead. Everyone seems happy that I'm joining their pack, and they're very friendly. A lot of people say that Jack and I look a lot alike, but I can't see it.

Jack told me that Ashton would officially accept me into the pack later that night, probably when we're alone. He said that it's calmer when the ceremony is more private.

Eventually everyone starts to leave after saying hello to me, and before I know it there are only a few people left standing around the dying fires.

I flop down on one of the legs, sighing in relief. My legs are killing me from standing up on them for so long.

Arms wrap around me and lift me up, making me yelp, before I'm settled on a familiar lap.

Ashton buries his face in my hair, his breath swirling down my neck. "You did great, angel." He coos, hands giving my hips a gentle squeeze.

I smile softly. "I like your pack."

"Our pack." He corrects.

I smile as I lean back against his chest.

Ashton reaches forwards around me and gently takes my left hand in his right one, pulling it diagonally across my chest and over my right shoulder. I turn to the side a little, so I'm not as twisted into such an awkward position.

"Ready to join my pack?" Ashton questions, his eyes sparkling.

I nod, smiling again.

He nods at me to.

As I watch I can physically feel his wolf leaping to the surface alongside the normal Ashton. His eyes flash gold, and his canine teeth elongate a little.

I watch as he opens his lips around my inner wrist. I can feel his sharper teeth scrape over the sensitive skin, making heat flare up and my stomach twist into strange knots. Out of nowhere he sinks his teeth into my wrist, making me hiss in a breath.

He swipes his tongue along my skin to clear away the blood. A shiver runs down his spine. He moves his mouth away from my wrist, lowering my hand into my lap.

'Can you hear me, angel?'

I jump at the voice inside my head, my eyes flying wide open. "Whoa!" I exclaim, staring at him strangely.

Ashton chuckles, gently grabbing my chin in his hand and bringing my face towards his. His lips meet mine as my eyes flutter closed for a moment.

Ashton smiles at me as he pulls away, hugging me closer. I can feel the joy radiating off him. He presses his face into the crook of my neck, making me giggle.

"Someone seems happy." I say, poking is head.

"Of course I am!" He replies, grinning. "My favourite girl has joined my pack. Why wouldn't I be happy?"

I blush as a smile curls at my lips. I grin and poke him in the side, making him flinch. His doe brown eyes look up to me for a moment, and I raise an eyebrow. A mischievous smile comes to my face as I realise someone is a little ticklish.

Ashton watches me with slight amusement running behind his features.

Grinning, I jab him in the sides again. Ashton flinches, yelping. I try not to laugh. But I can't help it.

"Oh, you think it's runny, do you angel?" Ashton smirks at me.

"Why yes, yes I do." I smirk back at him.

Ashton jumps at me, tackling me to the ground. I squeal as he easily pins me to the ground, straddling my hips. He puts his fingers into my sides and starts tickling me, making me shriek with laughter. I thrash under him as tears cloud my eyes.

"Ok, ok, I take it back!" I gasp in between breaths, trying to frantically push his hands away from me.

Ashton grins confidentially, sitting back and just watching me while I manage to get oxygen into my lungs. "Yeah, that's what I thought."

I grin, before putting all my effort into flipping us over so that I'm on top. "Just joking. I still think it's funny!" I tease, tickling him back.

Ashton starts laughing, trying to get me off him without hurting me. I giggle, pulling my hands back a little. "You owe me for going easy on you!" I chirp.

Ashton flips us over again, this time firmly pinning my hands beside my head. He lowers his lips down next to my ear, making my heart start pounding out of control. "It doesn't matter; I would do anything for you anyway."

A blush rises in my cheeks. I blink in surprise. He's so sweet... I grin up at him.

"Ok, so you remember what I told you about pack rules?"

"Yep!" I quip. "Obey the Alpha, respect other pack members, and protect the pack, right?"

Ashton smiles proudly, leaning back. "Perfect. Now with Mind Link, you have to keep up a wall if you don't want anyone hearing your thoughts. After a while it becomes natural, so your thoughts are pretty safe. Try to block me out."

"Ok." I say, before focusing. My brow furrows as I think I block my mind. It's kind of like a light switch in my brain.

Ashton smiles. "Good, that's it."

I giggle happily, and then try to wiggle out from under Ashton. I obviously don't get very far. "Ashton!" I whine. "Get off of me!"

"Hmm... no." He smirks.

I pout. "Meanie!"

"I'm not mean." He snorts.

"Then prove it. Get off me."

"No."

"Meanie!" I cry again.

He chuckles and I huff. "You're too cute." He teases, lightly tracing my cheekbone with his fingertips. I stare up at him in wonder as my face flushes.

Gently, Ashton leans down and presses his lips against mine. Like always, they're soft and warm and they make my heart race. His lips mould against mine perfectly, and it's very comforting. His body presses down against mine, pinning me to the ground.

Not that I'm moving anywhere anyway.

I giggle softly as Ashton nuzzles his face into the crook of my neck. I feel him breathe in my scent for a moment, before he lets out a satisfied grunt. He pulls me up with him, and wraps an arm around my waist tightly.

"C'mon, angel. I think it's time we head home."

"But what about the fires?" I question, tilting my head to the side as a frown creases my brow.

"One of the older pack members will put them out when they leave." Ashton explains, leading me across the field. Absentmindedly, he draws small circles on my hip.

"Ok." I chirp. "Do you know what time it is?"

He checks his phone. "About nine thirty."

"'Kay."

"When we get home, I want you to have a shower and go to bed, ok?"

"Aren't you gonna sleep to?"

He shakes his heads, making a sad look come to my face. "I just have to fill in some paperwork." He explains quickly. "I'll be there in about an hour, ok angel?"

Looking up at him, my eyes roll over his face before landing on his worried brown eyes. I find myself nodding my head, though the thought of sleeping in an empty bed is unwelcome. I know I can't stop Ashton from keeping up his Alpha duties, and I don't want to. His pack needs him more than I do.

I just wish there was something I could do to help, but I don't think there is.

At home, the room is empty when I walk in after having a brief shower. I quickly run a brush through my hair, which is getting really long now. I might have to get it cut, because it's hard to brush.

The bed feels even emptier. My bed is still in Ashton's room, but I don't use it unless it's just to lie on when Amy comes in and sprawls across the big one.

Crawling under the covers, I curl up and try to find warmth. I had gotten used to the heat from the bonfire, and from Ashton. Now there's nothing, no one but myself.

I pull my knees to my chest and close my eyes, wishing for sleep, and for Ashton.

(Ashton's POV)

Sighing, I finally put down my pen after reading through the last of the documents piled up on my desk. I didn't realise how much I actually had; it's well past midnight now.

I went to check up on Rosy a couple of hours ago, and I was relieved to find her asleep. I knew she was tired; meeting the pack was probably very emotionally draining for her. I admit, I did just stand at the doorway watching her for a moment.

Joshua's Father, the previous Beta, picks up the paperwork and files them in their appropriate places. Joshua was busy tonight, so Mr Daniels is helping me out instead. I don't feel right keeping Joshua up, let alone staying up this last myself, so having Mr Daniels to help out is a blessing.

"Thanks for your help." I say gratefully, slumping back in my chair.

"No problem, son." Mr Daniels chuckles, leaning against the filing cabinet. "Than new girl Rosalina is a stunner."

"Yeah, she is." I sigh airily, my mind wandering to my mate. "Gorgeous."

"She's fitting in well, isn't she?"

"Yeah."

"Jack seems glad she's back."

"Yeah."

"Amy seems glad to have a girl to talk to at home, too."

"Yeah."

"You really love your mate, don't you?"

"Yeah- wait, what?" I snap out of my daze just like that, turning to stare at Mr Daniels wide eyed. How did he...?

"Ashton, it couldn't be more obvious to a mated man like me. I recognised the way you practically drooled over Rosy. I was like that with my mate."

I look to the side, fighting off a blush. I'm a guy, I don't blush.

"So I'm guessing no one else knows." He crosses his arms at me. When I don't say anything, he sighs at me. "Not even Rosy?"

"How could she?" I sigh, rubbing my temples. "I don't know how to tell her. I really, really want to, but... how will she react? I don't even know how old she is mentally."

"I believe she's old enough." Mr Daniels says, his voice suddenly serious. "In her head, I mean. Tell her."

"I will." I say confidentially. "Just... not yet. She still doesn't know the truth about her parents, but I'm leaving that to Jackson."

He nods. "He should tell her soon though. A relapse wouldn't be healthy."

"Relapse?"

"It could happen." He says. "Though I doubt it."

I nod, feeling my heart flutter painfully. I can't help but worry for my angel.

"Well, I'm going to head home. You should get to bed to, Ashton. It's really late."

I nod, and stand up. "Thanks again for your help. I appreciate it."

"Anytime." He smiles. "You know me and Kaito were good friends."

At the mention of my Father, I smile bitterly. "Yeah, I know."

"Same with you and Josh." He smiles again, before turning and leaving. "Night. I'll lock the door on my way out."

"Thanks."

I wait until I hear the front door click shut, before standing and exiting the office. I stifle a yawn as I make my way upstairs, wanting to just curl up beside Rosy and fall asleep.

When I get to the room, I find Rosy trembling. Slight whimpers are tumbling past her opened lips, and sweat is covering her brow.

I freak out on the inside, and resist the urge to run over and shake her away and demand she tell me what's wrong. Instead, I calmly walk to our bed while peeling my shirt off and taking off my jeans.

Lying down, I wrap my arms around my little mate. "Rosy, c'mon darling', wake up." I say quietly, running my knuckles down her flushed cheek.

Rosy's eyes snap open as a petrified scream tumbles from her lips. Her eyes get watery before her bottom lip quivers and she starts to cry.

My heart aches as I scoop her up into my arms. "Shh, Rosy. Everything's fine. I'm here." I coo quietly, rocking her back and forth while stroking her messy hair flat.

Rosy grips tiny fistfuls of my hair as she wraps her arms around my neck. I rub her back gently as she stuffs her face in the crook of my neck, hot tears dripping onto my shoulder. I can't help but feel guilty for not being with her.

"I'm sorry, angel." I whine ruefully, pressing my lips against her forehead.

She sniffs, wiping away tears with a closed fist. Shaking her head, she mumbles, "P-please don't leave!"

I tighten my arms around her, feeling another wave of guilt hit me. "I won't." I vow.

Sniffling, Rosy lets her body slowly relax, muscle by muscle.

"Want to tell me what happened?" I ask softly, gazing at her tear-stained face. Absentmindedly I reach up and brush lingering tears away with my thumb. I let my hand cup her cheek.

"I... I had a nightmare." She whimpers.

"What about?" I coax.

"Can I ask you a question first?"

"Of course."

She turns her big blue eyes up at me, wiping away a single last tear. "What really happened to my parents?"

Chapter Twenty-Four

(Rosy's POV)

Clinging to Ashton, I watch him as he sleeps soundly. My mind wanders back to my nightmare.

I had seen my parents getting killed again. It's honestly quite terrifying.

Ashton just shook his head at my question, mumbling something about waiting until the morning. Its morning now, but he looks so happy asleep... I don't think I'll ask him about my parents again. The pained, guilty look he tried to hide from me made my heart ache.

I don't want someone I really like to feel like that.

Rolling over so that my back faces Ashton, I rest my head under my hand. I jump a little when Ashton reaches out and pulls himself up against my back. In his sleep, he nuzzles his face against the back of my neck and wraps his arm around my waist.

Sparks erupt all around my body. I sigh in content.

I study the picture on Ashton's bedside table. I've never really looked at it before; I always slept on the other side of the bed.

It's a picture of Ashton and his family. I recognise Linda and Amy. Linda is standing behind them with a man, who has his arms wrapped around her. Ashton is standing in front, with his arms over the shoulders of two girls. Amy is on his left, and another girl on his right. She looks a lot like Linda. They all wear matching grins that they flash at the camera.

I know the two I don't recognise must be Ashton's Father and his older sister, Diana. I think his Father's name is Kaito. I once heard Linda mention him, I think.

I can't help but let my mind wander back to my family. Besides for Jack, is there anyone else? Maybe from the pack my parents were in? What really happened to them?

Sighing to myself, I can't help but think Ashton and his family are very close. I'm not that close with Jack, which does bother me. I mean, he's my brother, right? So why don't I feel that close to him? Not to mention I feel like I've caused a rift between Ashton and Amy. They don't hang out much, and I bet they did a lot before I showed up.

Suddenly feeling extremely guilty, I curl up in on myself tighter and try not to cry.

It's Saturday, so Linda doesn't bother waking us up unless something big happens. It's already ten o' clock, and I was waiting for Ashton to wake up before I got up, but I think he was really tired last night.

Having me screaming and crying probably didn't help.

Bit by bit I pry Ashton's arm off of my waist, despite his unhappy growls. Thankfully he doesn't wake up, and I exit the room quietly.

Linda doesn't seem to be home when I make my way into the kitchen and find cereal. I find a note on the fridge though, explaining that she's gone out for the day.

I sit in the lounge room and watch Saturday morning cartoons while eating my breakfast quietly. Jack wanders down a little while later and flops down beside me.

"Morning, sis'."

"Morning." I answer quietly.

He looks at me out of the corner of his blue eyes. "What's wrong?"

"Nothing."

"Rosalina." His tone is a warning.

I place the now empty bowl on the coffee table and cross my legs. "It's just... I'm tired of this, you know?"

"'This'?"

I frown slightly. "It's all hitting home. I was out there for so long... I've missed so much..."

Jack sighs, and pulls me to his chest. "It's not your fault."

"I know that." I insist. "But I feel like I've intruded here."

"Rosy, you haven't intruded into anything. You're a welcome member of the pack, and you need to realise that."

I nod, though I don't believe him. I only joined the pack last night. A wolf is supposed to contribute to its pack, but there's nothing I can do at all.

I'm not strong, or fast, and no matter how much Ashton argues with me, I know deep down that I'm not worthy.

I'm starting to feel older than I should be.

Sighing, Jack stands up and reaches for his keys on the coffee table. "I'm going to head to work. You'll be ok until Ashton wakes up?"

"You work on a Saturday?"

"Sometimes. With the training going on in the pack at the moment, they need as many doctors as they can get." He chuckles.

"Yeah, I'll be fine." I nod, thinking hard. Training? Maybe I can do that...

Jack kisses my forehead, before leaving. I hear the front door shut behind me.

Slouching against the sofa, I tuck my legs under me and think of something to do.

Amy is out doing something with her friends, Jack is at work, Linda is out shopping, and Ashton is asleep. I think I need to make friends.

Sighing to myself, I resign to watching Tom and Jerry on the Saturday morning cartoons.

It's about an hour later when Ashton stumbles down the stairs, yawning. I bet he was up really late last night.

He doesn't notice me until he comes into the lounge room with vegemite toast. Blinking lazily at me, he walks over and plonks down next to me, eating his toast quietly. He yawns when he finished, placing his plate down on the coffee table. A moment later and he idly flops over so his head is resting in my lap.

"Are you tired?" I ask, tilting my head to the side as I run my fingers through his black strands. They're surprisingly soft.

He nods, eyes closed. "A little."

"Were you up late last night?"

Again he nods.

"Why?"

"I had more work to do than expected." He sighs, rolling over and hiding his face in my stomach. His breath makes a warm spot on my skin.

"Oh." It's all I can think of to say. I want to ask him about my parents again, but something feels wrong about it. I honestly don't know if I want the answer. Maybe I'll ask Jack later. He should know, right? "What are we gonna do today?"

I feel Ashton smile a little. "How about we gather everyone up and go to the beach?"

My mind flashes to the last time we went to the beach, just the two of us, and I can't help but grin. "Sure! I'll go find Amy!"

Ashton chuckles, sitting up as I bolt from the room.

It doesn't take long to gather up several people. There's Ashton, Amy, Mandy, Jack, Linda and Joshua. Linda is bringing along her friend, Rihanna, who's the same age as her. Joshua is also bringing along two friends, the twins Alex and Sage, who are twenty.

Overall, it's a fairly big group.

The beach is really sunny when we get there. A lot of human families are already around, but it doesn't bother anyone. We find a spot large enough for all of us, and then get to having fun.

Linda and Rihanna set up chairs and umbrellas, chatting. Jack and Mandy go off to find food for everyone, while Amy and I head straight for the water. Ashton, Joshua and the twins are further down the beach, tossing a football around.

The water is cold, but welcoming. Amy paddles around me in circles, looking bored. I flick water at her, grinning.

"What's up with you?" I question as she stands up, brushing water out of her eyes.

"Nothing." She grins. "Just wondering when I'll find my mate, is all."

"He'll pop up sooner or later."

She hums in response. "Jack and Mandy seem happy."

"Yep." I say, nodding. The two were always holding hands and smiling. "Mandy's really nice."

"Yeah. I'm glad he finally found his mate. Jack's the best doctor in the area, you know." Amy says, looking at me.

"Yeah, I know." I grin proudly, swishing my hands through the water. It comes up to my chest. "What was he like before he met Mandy?"

"Before he met Mandy, and before you showed up, he was pretty quiet." Amy says. "My Mum took him in when he was ten, after he showed up on our territory. He and Ashton got along really well."

"What happened when he appeared on your territory?" I ask curiously.

"Well... not much that I remember." Amy frowns a little. "I was pretty young, but I remember that it had been really quiet. I still don't really know what happened before Jack came to our pack."

"Oh." I answer. "So you don't know what happened to my parents?"

"Maybe you should ask Jack." Amy answers swiftly.

"But-"

"Rosy! Amy!" A voice calls out. I turn around to see Jack waving me and Amy to shore, while Mandy stands to the side waving at the guys. Guess the food is here.

The rest of the day went pretty smoothly. Ashton didn't question my nightmare, and I didn't bring my parents up again, to anyone. Once we all got home, Ashton, Amy and I went for a run before settling down and going to sleep.

The next morning I wake up before Ashton once again. I find myself sitting with a bowl of cereal, my eyes watching Tom and Jerry race around the screen.

I think I have a cartoon addiction.

Ashton wanders down a little while later and sits down next to me, yawning.

"What are we gonna do today?" I ask in between bites of cereal.

Ashton smiles a little. "Whatever you want. It's Sunday, but tonight we have something on, so try to think of something to do that won't clash with that."

"Um... I don't know." I admit with a shy grin. "What's happening tonight?"

"Just something." He yawns.

"Alright." I say, hiding my curiosity.

"Why don't you go out with Amy for the day?" Ashton suggest, sitting up.

"Huh?"

"You guys can have a girl's day out." Ashton continues, oblivious to my confusion. "Let me go talk to her."

And just like that, Ashton has left the room. I thought that we were going to do something together, like always. Well, I guess I can't always rely on Ashton, and hog his attention.

That thought sends a pang running down to my heart. The thought of another girl having Ashton's attention wants to make me cry. I quickly shake my head, dismissing the thoughts. I'm with Ashton, not another girl.

Focusing on the television again, I try to let the colourful cartoons take my attention away from worrying about my parents, and about Ashton's strange actions.

Amy wanders down the stairs a little while later, after several episodes of cartoons. We end up going shopping, where Amy squeals and coos over everything in every shop we pass. I can't focus, though.

What is Ashton up to?

Chapter Twenty-Five

(Rosy's POV)

Jack looks at me curiously. Sitting in my meadow, a place where I brought him, I can't help but grin and let the afternoon sunlight bore into my back. It's very warm.

"It's so peaceful here..." Jack sighs, leaning back on his hands.

"Yeah." I nod in agreement. "I like it here."

Jack looks at me, his familiar blue eyes glittering. The grass sways around us with the light breeze, seemingly uncaring.

"So how's Mandy?" I question.

A faint smile touches Jack's lips. "She's good. Great, actually."

Resting my chin in my palm, I stare at him pointedly. "So when are you getting married?"

"What?" He cries staring at me wide-eyed. I burst into a fit of giggles, clutching my stomach. His face - priceless. Though my question was serious, after all, don't mates get married quickly? They always fall in love straight away - it's almost impossible not to.

"It's ok, I was kidding. It's still too early, even for mates, right?" I laugh quietly.

Jack scowls, rubbing the back of his neck awkwardly. "You're such an evil child. Ashton's rubbing off on you." He whines.

I just grin. "You're so stupid."

He sighs, roll his eyes. "Whatever floats your boat."

I raise an eyebrow. He shrugs. I grin again.

"Jack?"

"Yeah?"

"What really happened to Mum and Dad?"

He blinks at me, shock registering on his face before he pales a little. For one long moment, he doesn't say anything. At first, I didn't think he would, but then he did.

Jack, for the first time, told me the truth about my parents - our parents. He told me about the house we lived in, and my favourite stuffed toy Miah, and he used to push me down the stairs just because he felt like it.

He told me about how every Tuesday was take-out night, and how the small pack we were a part of all gathered together to celebrate anything from birthdays to Christmases. He doesn't remember much about the other people in the pack, or who I was friends with, but he remembers that the Alpha was kind and powerful.

A solemn look passed over Jack's face as he continued on with his story. I didn't say anything, or let my face portray anything, as he told us about a pack of rogues that had been wiping out small packs at the time.

He tells me about the day our pack was attacked, despite us being so close to other much larger, more powerful packs. He tells me about how fires were started, and that all of our buildings were burnt down, including the pack house.

At that point, I had started to get a little teary, because I knew what was coming next. My nightmares had in fact been memories, not just mere dreams, because it was then that I realised I had witnessed the deaths of my parents.

Jack told me what he knew, from what he had seen and what he could remember. He had been separated from me and our parents in the chaos of the fires, and had escaped with a couple of the other pack members into the forest. Somehow, he had made it to Ashton's pack days later, after losing the other members, where Ashton and his family took Jack in and raised him to be the pack doctor he is today.

Ashton's father had sent out a search party, and they had found the bodies of all pack members - expect me. I was obviously alive, but they didn't know that. They thought I had died, or been taken, or that my body was in a location impossible to get to. If that wasn't the case, then they had not the slightest idea that had happened to me.

After that, Jack had driven me to the cemetery. The graves of our parents were located at the furthest corner of the rolling green field, under the shade of a blooming cherry blossom tree. Jack told me that it had been my favourite tree when I was little, which was why they were buried there. He said it was because it was like a tribute to me - whether I was alive or dead. He said I liked the tree because even though it only bloomed two weeks a year, it was by far the most beautiful.

He didn't know how a six year old had come up with that.

Frankly, I didn't either.

I had cried a lot. It was strange to comprehend the idea that I had been there when my parents had died - I had been so close to them. I found it almost repulsing that I had touched them when their bodies were turning cold, in fact, it was sickening. Sure, I didn't know at the time exactly what was happening, but it was still frightening.

Jack hadn't known that I had been there, so I told him about the nightmare, and he had realised.

His eyes had filled with tears, something I haven't seen ever happen to him, and he had been on the verge of crying.

I think in the end everything was better. I felt kind of relieved, like this weight that I hadn't ever noticed had been lifted off my shoulders. It cleared a lot of things up for me, and I felt like the rift between Jack and I had been fixed.

We stayed there for hours, and for once, I didn't feel like a young girl trapped inside an older body. I didn't feel like a child, and I didn't feel overwhelmed by this whole new world that was thrown at me. I didn't feel like the target of the rogues.

And to me, Jack didn't feel like the stranger who I used to know. He didn't feel distant, and he didn't feel too far out of my reach. He didn't feel foreign to me anymore.

For once, we were just older brother and younger sister, together ready to face the world.

I felt closer to him than I've ever felt before.

We had lunch at the local fish-and-chips shop. Jack kept me out all day, doing random things he said siblings should normally do when they're growing up. We went for a walk at a local park, and even fed the ducks in the lake.

They were pretty cute.

"Do you come here often?" I ask jack as I crouch by the edge of the pond, feeding a left over chip to a little brown duck.

"Yeah." Jack replies from his spot on a park bench just behind me. "Ashton and Linda showed me round the neighbourhood when I was younger. They used to take Amy here to feed the ducks."

"Ashton didn't feed them?"

Jack chuckles. "Not since one bit him, he doesn't."

I laugh, scaring one of the crowding ducks who flaps his wings at me. I throw another chip into the shallow water. "Why'd it bite him?"

"Who knows?"

"Maybe the duck didn't like him."

"Probably. It was worse for him when the duck took bread off Amy straight afterwards, though."

I laugh again. "Poor Ashton."

"Yep."

"When are we going home?" I ask, feeding the last of the chips to the ducks before throwing the rubbish in a nearby bin.

"What, am I boring you?" Jack teases me.

"No! It's just that I feel like everyone is up to something." I say as he stands and we start walking back towards his car.

"Hmm? No, I don't think so."

"Oh? I think you're in on it to." I grin at him sneakily, elbowing him in the ribs and making him yelp, tough probably not from pain.

"Think what you want, little Rosy dear, but I'm not saying a word." A sly grin covers his face, giving it a happy glow.

It was nice.

You know, seeing him this happy. Jack's always been happy, sure, especially since Mandy is around now. A mate can make anyone happy.

I know for a fact that Jack is even happier now. He's always smiling around her, kissing her cheek, holding her hand. His eyes always sparkle when Mandy's in the room.

Mandy is the same way too. She's fit right into the pack, settling straight away. She doesn't complain about Jack's strange work hours, and how much of a burden I was all those weeks ago. Anyone else and they would have been fed up with me, but Mandy... she's so nice and patient that she didn't care. I bet she'd make a good mother one day!

They make a perfect pair.

Jack leads me back to his car.

Getting in, I buckle my seatbelt and relax against the soft seat covers. A small rear-mirror charm hangs in the air between us, glittering when the sun hits it in the right position. It looks like some sort of tribal sun, and glows orange to match the colour of the setting sun.

I snap out of my little retrieve as Jack starts the car. Pulling out of the park's parking lot, we start on the drive home.

By the time we pull into the driveway, the sun has almost disappeared completely from the sky, dipping down behind the horizon.

Heading inside, I'm shocked to find that the lights are all off. "It's dark..." I say loud enough for Jack to hear as he walks in behind me.

"Turn on the light then."

Nodding, mostly to myself, I feel along the wall until my fingers comes across the light switch. I flick it on, and light floods into the lounge room.

"Surprise!"

A startled cry escapes my lips as everyone I've met since I've been here jumps out of various hiding spaces, like behind the couches and from around the corner. My eyes widen at the sight of all the coloured balloons, the bowls of food and the bright banner that wishes me a happy seventeenth birthday.

Jack grins, ruffling my hair as I stand there gawking. "Happy birthday, little sis."

Tears cloud my eyes as a big grin splits across my face. "Thank you all so much!"

A collective chuckle of laughter echoes around the room, before soft music gets played in the background and everyone starts talking with each other.

My eyes scan the room until I find who I'm looking for.

Ashton walks over to me with a warm smile on his handsome face. Wrapping me up in his arms, I'm instantly comforted by his intoxicating scent. "Happy birthday, my angel." He murmurs, smiling.

"Thank you." I say, standing up on my toes to give him a kiss on the cheek.

The rest of the night goes smoothly. This was the reason Ashton was acting so strange; I don't know why I didn't see it before.

After a sit down dinner with everyone, I'm given presents. I was astounded by how many nice things people bought for me I would have been happy with a card. Most of the things I got I was missing, though, like clothes I could wear and books I could read. Linda even gave me a mobile phone, and I have a feeling it is going to take a while to figure out, but I was thankful nonetheless.

Ashton's present was my favourite.

He gave me a ring, with his name engraved on the inside of it. I think I started crying again, and Linda just had to take at least a dozen photos. Ashton showed me that he had a matching one, and it even had my name in it.

It was then that I realised just exactly what Ashton meant to me.

I think I started laughing. It got his attention, because he thought I was laughing at his gift, but I knew it wasn't that. I was laughing because I felt stupid, which I told him, because I never realised he was my mate.

I had a feeling that my life was going to be fine from then on.

Epilogue

(Rosy's POV)

"Kaito!" I cry, laughing so hard tears stream down my face. "Stop, please!"

I hear an all too familiar chuckle as Ashton swoops in, plucking the six-year-old ball of energy off my protruding stomach.

The blonde boy gets a mischievous grin on his face, reaching out slightly chubby hands for me. Of course I hold my arms out, letting him fly from Ashton's grip into mine, careful of my stomach. Kaito grins as Ashton rolls his eyes, sticking his tongue out childishly.

"Ha!" Kaito cries, rubbing his cheek against my own. "Mummy loves me better!"

Ashton pouts as I laugh quietly. It's always been like that with our son - he's a complete Mummy's boy. As for Finnian, who we just call Finny, he was the complete opposite. He won't leave Ashton's side other than to sleep.

It's so adorable.

I couldn't be happier with the way my life has turned out. Ten years after my seventeenth birthday, and I'm a happily married Alpha Female with two beautiful boys and a third child on the way.

I can still remember when Ashton proposed. I had attended an actual school for year twelve, and I had done very well. It was hard at first, being away from my mate, but I had adjusted and made a lot of friends. It was cute, because Ashton constantly worried.

Anyway, after graduation Ashton took me out on a picnic to my meadow. He had personally cooked everything... with Linda's help. Later, when the stars were finally out, he casually took my hand, told me why he loved me and asked me to marry him.

A year and a half later and I was walking down the aisle in white, with Jack at my side. He and Mandy had been married sixth months earlier, which is why Ashton and I postponed our own ceremony. At the time, Mandy was seven months pregnancy with twin girls.

The ring Ashton gave me was beautiful. It sat on my finger with the engagement ring, which I refused to take off. The ring for my seventeenth birthday was safely strung on a chain that hung around my neck.

A year and a bit later, on my twenty-first birthday, I told Ashton I was pregnant.

He had fainted.

It was hilarious. I couldn't stop laughing, and neither could anyone else. It didn't take long for him to wake up, and despite being embarrassed, he was ecstatic. I've never seen him smile like that, other when the time I was walking down the aisle.

Nine months later and Kaito arrived. It took forever, and it really hurt, but it was worth it. Linda burst into a torrent of tears when Ashton and I told her we had named our first son after her husband, Ashton's father.

At first, it was really stressful taking care of a newborn baby. By then, I was acting and thinking like any twenty-one year old, but it's stressful for any first time mother, so I knew my reactions were natural.

I couldn't stop staring at Kaito, and I loved who small and little he was. With thick blonde hair and blue eyes, just like me, he was loved by everyone in the pack almost instantly.

Two years after that and Finny was born. He was smaller than Kaito when he was born, and a month premature and I was so frazzled that it took Ashton ages to finally get me to relax. I was terrified I had done something wrong, and I became very possessive of Finny. I wouldn't let any of the pack members, despite how much I knew and loved them, to hold him for months.

They understood though. I was very thankful of that.

Finnian, like Kaito, also had my thick blonde hair. But his eyes were completely Ashton's - that deep chocolate brown that everyone instantly falls in love with. We named Finnian in memory of my father.

Now, four years after Finnian was born, and I'm twenty-seven. My life couldn't be better.

Ashton and I live in our own house, within the pack territory. We use the pack house as, well, a housing place for any wolf that wants it.

I went to university and became a music teacher at the local primary school, teaching both wolves and human children. I love my job, and I seem to be very popular with the students. Kaito's always so proud to say that Miss Rosy is his Mum.

This is also Finny's first year of kindergarten. He looked so adorable in his little uniform, and reminds me so much of Kaito.

"So," Ashton says, flopping down to occupy the spot on the soft sofa beside me, "How are my lovely ladies feeling?" He asks, wrapping his arms around my waist and placing his hand flat against my stomach.

We found out we were having a girl two weeks ago.

"Good. Hungry." I answer with a bright grin as Finny waddles into the room, a bucket full of toy cars clutched against his chest.

"Kaito, play cars with me!" He whines, his childish voice sounding younger with his slight lisp on the 'r' and 'w' sounds.

Kaito pouts, his eyebrows drawing together. He doesn't want to, that is plain enough to see, but he's so protective of his brother that he'll do anything Finny wants.

"Fine, but you owe me!" Kaito decides, clambering off the sofa and onto the floor where Finny has upended the bucket and tipped the cars onto the rug.

"Ok, help me up." I say, holding my hands out to Ashton.

He grins, standing up and gently lifting me to my feet. Placing my hands on the small of my back, I make my way to the kitchen in search of a lot of food just as someone rings the doorbell.

"I'll get it!" I hear Kaito screech before his footsteps echo down the hallway.

"W-wait for me!" Finny scrambles after him, latching onto Ashton's leg as he goes after them. I don't really like them answering the door by themselves, just in case there is some stranger on the other side, so Ashton always goes with them, or I do.

As I rifle through the lower cupboards, I faintly hear the boys opening the door to their grandma. Linda always comes over to visit; she can hardly stay away. I don't mind, she loves to babysit the boys so Ashton and I can have some alone time.

"Momma, Grandma is here!" Kaito chirps happily as he barrels into the room, half tackling my legs.

I grin down at him. "Oh, is she now?"

"Of course I am!" Linda cries, coming into the room with Finny in her arms and Ashton carrying her purse. The sight is funny, and makes me laugh.

"That purse suits your eyes, love." I tease, running my fingers through Kaito's silky locks.

He rolls his eyes at me. "Aren't you supposed to be eating?"

My eyes widen. "Oh yeah! But I can't reach the top shelf." I say, pursing my lips as I stare at the cupboard. I haven't grown much these last ten years, and I find myself straining to reach the higher cupboards even without the whole swollen stomach.

"Ha." Ashton teases back, putting his mother's purse on the counter. I pout, crossing my arms childishly.

"Ashton!" Linda chastises, scowling unhappily. "Your wife is carrying your child and you won't help her? I thought I raised you better than that!"

Kaito bursts out laughing at Ashton's frightened face, clutching his stomach. "Daddy's being naughty and he got told off!" He laughs. His laughter makes Finny burst into a fit of adorable little giggles that he tries to hide behind his small hands.

Ashton gapes. "Why am I always getting scolded in this family?"

I couldn't help but beam at that word. Family. It's what we are. "Aw, poor darling."

He sniffles, playing up the whole woe-is-me part. Slinking forwards Ashton cuddles into my side and nuzzles his face into my neck. He's so damn tall he has to hunch over, but that never seems to deter him.

"You're such a big baby." I giggle quickly, patting his head as I let his warmth envelope my little body.

"But you love me anyway." He sighs dreamily in return, giving me his signature dazzling grin. Even after all these years, that smile of his can still make me weak at the knees.

Probably not the best thing for a heavily pregnant woman to be.

Ashton straightens up and places a chaste kiss on my lips, before turning to the cupboard with a determined look. "Ok, what do you want?"

"What's up there?" I question, clinging onto his arm as I attempt to stand on my toes.

Attempt being the operative word. My feet were so swollen from carrying around this baby that it was difficult just standing.

"Just get everything." Linda suggests as she pulls out colourful crayons and paper from one of the bottom draws, placing them on the small table at the other end of the kitchen. We bought it for the boys, because they didn't like it when Ashton and I were in a different room, especially with Linda around.

"Good idea." Ashton says, easily pulling down anything edible from the cupboard.

"Rosy you should sit down before you give yourself worse backaches. Let me go and get a couch pillow." Linda says, knowing that the kitchen stools hurt my bottom and back.

I watch in silent amusement as Kaito leads Finny over to the table by the hand and gets him the coloured crayons he asks for. They're so endearing that it makes my heart warm.

Linda comes back in the room a moment later, a plump cushion in her hand. She puts it on one of the stools and helps me waddle my way onto it.

"Thanks." I say, sighing as relief floods my legs. Being pregnant wasn't one of the most comfortable things in life, especially not with rearing, kicking werewolf pups. "Are Jack and Mandy coming over?"

"They should be here soon." Linda answers. "They're bringing Cindy and Wendy, as well."

"Cool." I answer, covering my mouth as an unexpected yawn surfaces. The twins were about a year older than Kaito, and had Mandy's light hair that was browner than blonde and Jack's blue eyes. The two of them always wore matching clothes, at their own choice. Like two peas in a pod.

"What would you like to eat, angel?" Ashton questions, looking at me with those doe brown eyes and a curious expression.

My heart flutters like it always does when he looks at me like that; like I'm the most precious thing in the world to him. "Hmm... anything with chicken." I answer, reaching a hand forwards to rub my stomach. "I like chicken."

He chuckles. "I know. You've seemed to love it more since the baby." He gestures towards my stomach, turning back to the freezer.

I sigh. "That's cravings for you."

Ashton chuckles once more.

Things go smoothly that night. Jack and Mandy arrive halfway through Ashton cooking me several meals of chicken, Cindy and Wendy in tow. They join my kids in a game of hide and seek, running around the house like the energetic children they are.

The adults - Jack and Mandy, Linda and Ashton and I - all chat, talking about things like the next pack bonfire and what colour Ashton and I should paint the new nursery.

The topic of the rogues briefly surfaces, but it's quickly dismissed.

After that last attack on the pack when I was still sixteen, the rogues seemed to back off for a while. Two years after and Ashton had formed a treaty with a strong pack nearby - the Alpha's son was friends with me during year twelve, and we had become close. He got along with Ashton great, and there was no jealousy or spitefulness between them.

Besides, Alfie was quite delightful to be around. With curly golden locks and bright caramel eyes, I was surprised that he didn't have a mate or partner.

Anyway, the rogues attacked when I was eighteen and our pack, along with Alfie's pack, wiped them out clean.

We never learnt why they were after me.

I don't really want to know. I had a feeling it had something to do with my parents, maybe something that they never spoke to anyone of, but I was not going to allow their misfortune to hurt Jack or I anymore, especially not with our families growing and prospering so much.

Then, about nine o' clock, I felt a sharp stab of pain shoot through my waist that made me double over. I'd been through it twice before; I knew the baby was coming.

At least Ashton didn't faint this time, though he looked pretty queasy. I had to tell him what to do, and it was quite amusing considering he's supposed to be the all-mighty tough alpha in this relationship.

Everyone rushed me to the hospital so fast I barely had any time to organise things. I had already placed an emergency bag in the car with things that I'll need, like spare clothes and baby things.

Linda would be in the waiting room with the boys, as well as Mandy and the twins. Jack would deliver the baby - he was honoured when I asked him to do it for Kaito and Finny, so I figured this baby was no different. He was still an exceptional doctor- and was even now known throughout the country and the werewolf communities.

Like always, the smell of the hospital irritates my nose. Alfie arrives in the nick of time as I'm wheeled into the operation room - he's kind of like my midwife.

I have to say, labour is probably the most painful thing I've ever gone through. But after the hours and hours of excruciating pain, screaming, whining and the casual glares aimed at Ashton, everything is forgotten because I'm holding a new life in my arms.

"She's beautiful." Ashton murmurs, half lying on the hospital bed beside me. He sounds oddly tired as he gazes down at the pink bundle in my arms.

I chuckle weakly. "Why are you tired? I'm the exhausted one here."

Ashton smiles to himself, brushing hair away from my sweaty forehead. "What do you want to call her?" He asks me.

"I don't know." I admit softly, letting out a yawn. The baby lets out a small yawn, making me laugh quietly. Like mother, like daughter. "What about you?"

Ashton shakes his head.

I stare down at our daughter. Her skin was pale and soft, two pink splotches colouring her chubby cheeks. Black hair just like Ashton's covered her head in curls similar to mine. Calm blue eyes give her an innocent look.

"Lisanna." I say.

Ashton smiles. "Lisanna... perfect."

I smile too, resting against the pillows and shifting until I get into a more comfortable position. "I wouldn't mind giving her Diana as a middle name." I say.

Ashton's eyes widen for a moment, a teary look coming to his face. "Are you sure?" He asks, his voice almost scratchy.

I nod happily. Naming my daughter after Diana would be an honour, especially since Ashton was so close to his late older sister.

Ashton places a loving kiss on my forehead. "Thank you, angel. I would love that..."

"Lisanna Diana." I muse. "I love it."

"Agreed." Ashton nuzzles his face into the crook of my neck.

A soft sign escapes my lips. I was exhausted, and all I wanted to do was sleep, but I wanted to see my family's reaction to our little Lisanna.

A knock on the door has Ashton and me looking up. Jack pops his head in, looking just as tired as I am. He looks at me expectantly, and I nod. He opens the door wider, letting everyone in.

The first person I see is Kaito. Of course, the little bundle of energy dives straight into the room, clambering up onto the bed and into my lap.

"Mummy!" He cries, though his voice is whispery - Linda probably told him to be quiet when he came in. "Are you better now, Mummy?"

I chuckle, absentmindedly rocking Lisanna in my arms. "Yes, honey."

Next I see Finny stumbling his way through the adults. He practically tackles Ashton's legs, burying his face there as his little fists grip Ashton's jeans. He lets out a childish whine, pouting miserably as he clings to Ashton.

As I said before, he hardly ever leaves Ashton's side.

Ashton reaches down and picks him up, giving him a view of me and Lisanna. His curious eyes scan the bed, before he puts on a satisfied expression and buries his face in the crevice of Ashton's neck.

Linda follows them into the room, with Mandy and the twins behind her.

"Wow." Linda gasps breathlessly, peering at Lisanna's peaceful face. "She's so beautiful."

"We named her Lisanna." Ashton provides, holding Finny on his hip. "Lisanna Diana."

Linda's eyes go wide as tears cloud them. She looks at me, and tries to form words, but ends up just crying and throwing her arms around me.

I laugh quietly. "Want to hold her?"

Linda nods, holding her hands in front of her mouth before opening her arms. I carefully place Lisanna in them, wary of not bumping her head. Linda coos down at her while Kaito climbs into my arms, resting his head against my chest. He'd done that since he was born, so it was normal for me to sit still as he listens to my heartbeat.

"She's gorgeous." Mandy praises, her arms around Cindy and Wendy as she holds them against her body. Jack nods in agreement, his arms around Mandy as he touches Lisanna's cheek gingerly.

"Thanks." I say around a yawn, resting my head on top of Kaito's. His hair is so soft it makes me sleepy.

The family stays for a while, before Jack leads everyone out. Ashton holds Lisanna for a while as Kaito and Finny fall asleep on the small couch set up in the room. Ashton eventually sets Lisanna down in the small crib provided for new babies, before squeezing in beside me and wrapping me in his arms.

Its times like these that I savour.

Things have turned out perfect for me. I wouldn't change anything even if I could. I love my pack, I love my family, I love my children and I love my mate.

I sigh, nuzzling into Ashton's warm chest like I always have. He still has the most intriguing scent and the most dazzling smile - well, besides Kaito's cheeky grin that he got from his Father.

"Love you." I yawn quietly, kissing the underside of Ashton's chin.

Ashton tightens his arms around me and presses his lips my forehead. "Love you too, angel."

www.ingramcontent.com/pod-product-compliance
Lightning Source LLC
Chambersburg PA
CBHW072152070526
44585CB00015B/1099